MESSAGE FROM THE MOUNTAIN

Awakening to Your Life's Purpose

By

Chuck Gallagher

Message from the Mountain
Awakening to Your Life's Purpose

http://chuckgallagher.com

Dedication

This book is dedicated to my wife Deborah, who is an inspiration for my Spiritual journey, and my two sons, Rob and Alex, who each through their uniqueness continue the journey of "Little Feather" and "One Who Flies."

Table of Contents

Preface

At times in life, there are chance happenings that, when reflected upon, are revealed to be turning points—times when life changes and what we know, or what we think we know, is substantially altered. The words that follow are the simple expression of one of those times for me—a time that lasted for two years—a time of substantial spiritual growth.

As I stumbled down the stairs that fall night in Raleigh, NC, fired up the laptop, and began to write, I had no idea what would follow. As far as I knew, I was writing just to get "stuff" off my mind so I could finally fall asleep. Sleeping had never been an issue for me, so it was unnerving to find it difficult to fall asleep that night. Something had to be done about it, and, at my stage of life, writing seemed the only practical medicine for the restless night that I was experiencing.

Sitting down at the keyboard in the dark of night was certainly not typical for me, but the actions that followed—well, they were like none that I had ever experienced before.

I recall placing my fingers on the keyboard, closing my eyes and typing. At that moment, time seemed to stand still. It was as if there was a voice inside my head that directed my fingers, and soon I found the beginnings of a story, some parts drawn from real life and others from an inspired reality that came as naturally as breathing. There was no plan, no structure, certainly no thought. It was as if, in the cosmic universe, I was just a portal through which words and feelings took form and from which I began to find answers to questions I hadn't known I had.

As I write this Preface—looking back over this incredible writing experience—I have come to know that messages come to us all. The question is not, "Do we receive messages?" Rather, the question is, "How do we receive them, and are we open to receiving them?" Whether they come in the form of a burning bush, a still small voice or, as in my case, a really sleepless night, the fact is that when we are ready to receive our message(s), the messenger will appear.

Perhaps, as you take this journey with me, you will find a way to connect with your messenger. She's out there. Sometimes we just have to be sleepy—and yet restless—enough to listen.

Chapter One

The Voice

S eldom, if ever, was she seen—at least, that's what I was told later. Where she lived was a mystery, as well. I'd never seen her, not in real life, but it was said that she would only appear when the one to which she wanted to speak was ready to listen. The locals said that the old woman from the mountain didn't speak often, but when she spoke, her words were full of truth and wisdom.

Like an inner voice, the question was, *Will I listen?*

"Mother Earth reveals what you need to know when it's time. Everything has a season," said a whisper in the wind as the golden maple leaves began to fall all around in the crystal fall air.

Something deep within the mountain was calling me, and I knew that this was an important time—a time to listen and learn. Something was speaking to me. Perhaps, this time, the voice was stronger. Perhaps, this time, I was ready to hear. But something deep within was calling me to be still and know.

I first heard the call as I drove from west to east, climbing higher into the depth and height of the eons-old Great Smoky Mountains. There was something different this time. I knew that I felt at peace in the mountains, but never had I been more aware of just how much emotion I could feel than this year when the summer gently rolled into fall.

It was as if the vibration was different, more intense. The armor that had protected me for so long had done its job, and now it was time to slowly remove it. I didn't know it, but perhaps it wasn't needed any more. Finally, after such a very long time, I was beginning to breathe again, and I knew that it was time to listen to the woman from the mountain. Her message was important to hear. Her message would save my life.

Crisp—that's how I would describe the air. Deep within my lungs, I could feel its life force in a body that had been worn somewhat by time and choices. Somehow, as she spoke, all my senses were heightened. The sounds of birds flying up above seemed clear, as the migration to escape the harshness of winter had begun.

Gentle white clouds seemed to drift aimlessly by as I noticed a sky that was nothing but Carolina blue—the kind of sky that might be seen in Montana, Wyoming, or areas far away from the speed of life. This time, the sky revealed its clarity in the height and breadth of the Great Smoky Mountains.

"It all happens for a reason, these changes." Her voice was clear, yet tempered with the compassion of age. There was a cadence to the rhythm of her words, even to her breathing. It was as if she was in perfect sync with the vibration of the mountain—as if she had been there for many lifetimes. Yet, as I heard her words, I still could not see the one who spoke.

"Listen. What do you feel?"

Five simple words, and yet they were so hard to answer. I could tell that time with the old woman would bring about changes, perhaps some for which I was unprepared.

My feelings were stuffed away deep within and taught never to surface. That is, after all, why the armor had been so well crafted over the years. I was content living within the armor. Through many battles, it had done its job. Now, as she asks about feeling, I experience a loosening of the armor. Inside, I felt a certain fear knowing that, as I entered this new phase, I would be vulnerable.

Her words again rang in my head but, this time, I seemed to notice that they started in my heart: "What do you feel?"

With those words, I began to feel tightness in my throat as my eyes began to well up with tears. *Emotion*, I thought, trying to pull the armor tight around me to suppress the feeling in favor of thought. Seems I was good at that. As long as I stayed in my head, I didn't have to deal with matters of the heart. My armor—my head—had been an effective protective mechanism for most of my life. Somehow, as I felt her words, I knew that was about to change. Life was entering a new phase—a new transformation.

Things felt different here. Life was somehow slower. It was as if you could feel another time. Somehow—although it was foreign to my head—it seemed I could sense the souls of many who had passed before me. On one level, it was as if I was not alone. Yet, at the same time, I felt more alone here than at any time in my recent past.

My head always made sure that I was protected—surrounded by people, things and experiences. I had created a cornucopia of distractions that kept my mind occupied, protecting me from the depth of feeling that it was now time to experience. Was I truly ready?

As if reading my mind, the woman spoke: "Feel the breath of the mountain." She spoke with a loving, gentle voice, quietly in the recesses of my mind. "Drink it in, and feel."

I knew clearly what she was talking about. From nowhere, I felt for the first time the profound sense of being alone. I felt a sharp pain as emotion welled up from deep within. A quiet scream seemed to come from inside me declaring, "I am." Yet, as if from the quietest place, I felt a profound sadness, knowing that no one heard. No one heard, and the tears flowed and expressed years of pain.

"Good. You feel. That is good."

I could tell that the old woman from the mountain knew that her time with me would not be in vain. The armor was loosened enough to allow for a new phase of life to start. Perhaps, if I focused deeply enough on my heart, I would be open to the feeling that was to come and the message I was to hear. Perhaps someone would notice—"I am!" Perhaps that someone is me.

With my eyes closed, the crystal clear air dancing around my head, her rich warm voice, steeped with the wisdom of the ages, began. "It is your time," she said. I heard the words, but I also felt love as she spoke them.

"Sit. We will be here for a while. There is much to feel. There is much to learn. The circle of life is not over for you." I heard those words not only in my head but also through my being, and I knew that, if I missed the message, any meaningful life for me would be over. It was time to be still and open my senses to what was coming. "I am" depended on it.

As, once again, the clear air filled my lungs, I waited on what the old woman from the mountain was to say.

Chapter Two

The Question

"Who are you?"

The old woman from the mountain asked this simple question with a forceful kindness, as if summoning something that would come from deep within.

Before I could answer audibly, I felt the answer that I did not wish to speak: "I do not know." *I dare not say that,* I thought as I tried to formulate my answer in my head. *Surely I could define myself with…*

"That's correct. You do not know. Very good."

She had responded to my answer before I could come up with an answer. How? I was always quick with my head. Yet, her ability to hear my heart and respond before I could answer unbalanced me. The experience was unfamiliar. Before I spoke an answer or even came up with something I thought was plausible, the old woman from the mountain responded.

"You feel the truth," she explained.

As she spoke those words, it seemed that I no longer needed to hear them audibly—although she spoke them aloud. There was a power with her truth. The words were simple, yet their truth had a perfect resonation within my body. I didn't have to guess at her thoughts or feelings. She spoke, and I knew—that was all.

"You have always known your true answers," she continued. "You have just chosen to hide them—and hide them so well that now you find it hard to distinguish between the truth and the fiction in your head."

I knew as she spoke the words that they rang full of truth. My keenly tuned mind was quick to respond to people so that I spoke the words they needed to hear. Mentally understanding a person, sensing their needs and asking the right questions, had become easy. I could effortlessly redirect any question asked of me as a question back to the one who asked. I was a master illusionist. Not only had my armor protected me from direct attack, but also it kept most—if not all—from knowing what was protected within. Few, if any, knew me!

It seemed as if I could feel the crisp gentle breeze blow through the old woman's long grey hair. Perhaps it was just my mind trying to take over again—or maybe I was really feeling through her? Yet, somehow, the breeze provided a kind of clearing, perhaps a new beginning. It was hard to understand what was taking place, but the message seemed clear and important.

Again, knowing the struggle within, and with a love and kindness that I'd last felt from my grandmother, she asked, "Who are you?"

By this time, my mind had recovered from the first time she'd asked this question, and now it seemed easier to answer. "I am a…"

"Are you feeling your answer?" she asked with a quiet firmness. The breeze again stirred as if to say, "Feel me, and feel yourself. It is time to feel."

As I'd begun to speak my answer, I had not noticed that there was no feeling. My head was in full control as I had begun to say, "I am a VP of Sales." Perhaps it is different for each of us, but I could not recall when I had defined myself by anything other than the job or title I carried. I suppose that is not so uncommon, as men in the past took their surnames from their occupations. Whatever the justification, I had chosen from the beginning of my adult years to define myself by the function I performed. It was as if my value was only defined by what

I did, not who I was. But the question was, "Did I know who I was? Really?"

Again, with a sound of heaven in her voice, the old woman from the mountain felt my thoughts and responded. "That's what we're here to help you learn: the true answer to the question. Who are you?"

"Your journey may take you to unexpected places," she stated. "It will force you to find stillness and to listen from within. Are you willing to go there?" Her question was asked with respect, acknowledging that I had the will to choose whether I would go into uncharted waters or live the rest of my life bound by the rusting armor I had created.

"We will find a rock and sit for a while." Her loving voice made it easy to move forward. My guess was she had done this before, perhaps many times over many lifetimes. I had the sense that she was the spirit guide of inner knowing, but she did not reveal that part of herself to me. All I could truly feel was the love she felt as she guided me through the process.

As the sun warmed my face, I sat still on the rock. Its semi-flat surface was weathered. Somehow I knew that the rock had been there for millions of years, gently providing its vibration as a place for the weary to sit and ponder. The golden rays seemed to kiss my cheeks with love and warmth, my body contoured to the rock's firm foundation, and time seemed to change. The vibration of what was around me was absorbed in nature. While the mind could become cluttered with thought, disturbing the harmony, with stillness the clarity of feeling was possible.

"Rest for now," she said, "as the journey to soul discovery will take time. Piece by piece, we will need to lovingly remove your battle armor. Then you will begin to come to fully know the grandeur of who you are. You want to know, right?"

As I felt the question resonating through my body, I also felt some level of fear and trepidation. Mostly, though, I felt excitement about the joy that would follow. I was unsure about the journey, but I knew that the old woman from the mountain would lead me with love. We would only go as far and fast as I was willing to feel and receive.

She was right, however, in her direction. It was now time to rest.

Chapter Three

The First Steps

"It's time to wake up from your mind sleep."

As I heard the words ring clear from the old woman from the mountain, I felt refreshed as if I had been resting for hours. Yet, as I observed all that was around me, I came to understand that my time on the rock had been only minutes—perhaps thirty at most. The sun was moving west into mid-afternoon, and the breeze that had caressed my cheeks so gently just hours earlier began to increase in intensity as if to signal something new was blowing into my life.

My 'mind sleep....' Her last words replayed again in my head. I wanted to shake my head, as her words seemed to create a sense of imbalance within me. *Their meaning may not be as clear as I first hear them*, I thought.

"You are right," she uttered. "My words have a deeper meaning for you."

Her voice came from nowhere. Not once had I spoken a word of my thoughts.

"You will learn. Thoughts do not have to be spoken to have power. Your thoughts, whether spoken or not, have tremendous power. I will guide you based upon the truth of your thoughts."

As the crisp breeze began to swirl around my head, the words I heard framed my next steps and explained why my mind felt so unbalanced. As uncomfortable as the feeling of imbalance was, it seemed that my spirit guide—this old woman from the mountain—was encouraging me to feel more than think. So, I suppose I could only expect that my lessons would move me out of my comfort zone.

With a gentle sternness, the old woman from the mountain spoke clearly. As I heard the words, I knew that this was just the beginning of a new journey and I should listen with more than just my ears.

"Waking up from your mind sleep—did you hear what I said to you earlier?"

"Yes, but what did that…." before I could finish my question, she emphatically stepped back in, letting me know that she was in control here.

"You have been in a mind sleep for too long. Clear your head! Hear me. I am not talking about sleep as you understand it. You think of it one way—you see the obvious. Seeing the obvious is 'mind sleep.' You walk around, talk with people, and carry on your business, yet your mind is asleep. You are missing life as it swirls around you—too focused on what you think is important and missing the vibrancy of life. When you free your mind of useless clutter, you will begin to wake up from your 'mind sleep.'"

Wow, I thought, *that's the most I've heard her speak since we met.* As if from nowhere—yet also from everywhere—I heard her once again, her voice softening in tone.

"The more you analyze what I say, like you just did, the more deeply you find yourself in 'mind sleep.' It's time to wake up. Here's the question you might be asking yourself: How did you feel when I said to you what I said? Your feelings are your guide to truth in your life, not your analysis of how much or little I may say to you.

"Wake up from your mind sleep!"

What she said resonated with me, although I certainly was not accustomed to observing my feelings or, better said, feeling my feelings. Yet I knew that what she said was right. The first thing I did was analyze the magnitude instead of truly hearing and understanding what she said.

It's strange how quickly and easily truth resonates. As I sat upright on the weathered rock, watching the sun slowly drop to the horizon, I chuckled to myself. How foolish. Often in the past, I would be introduced to someone in a business meeting, then turn around, and when I looked back at him or her, I couldn't recall his or her name. It was as if I was walking in a fog, my mind jumping from one idea to the next, yet none of it really connecting to the life that was taking place around me. The things that seemed important at the time were soon forgotten, memories replaced with nothing—time seemingly wasted.

Perhaps for too long I have been in this "mind sleep." *But then again,* I thought, *what if this is the way it's supposed to be.* As soon as that thought was formulated in my brain, I once again got a response that I had not asked for.

"You think too much. Do you recall what I asked you earlier?"

Honestly, as she asked me that question, I could not recall; I was too caught up in the "mind sleep" comment to recall much more of what had been said. I was doing exactly what she had suggested I shouldn't do—analyze with my mind, seeking the obvious.

"Of course you don't," she said, "but I do. I asked you who you were. Do you recall now?"

"Yes," I replied, not sure where this was going.

"You could not answer that question. You tried, but in the end, when you began to feel, you had no response. But, to your credit, you did feel, and that was good.

"When you felt the sadness, that was one of the first times that you disconnected from your keen mind and connected to life that goes on around you. You did not know who you are, and you still don't. Yet that moment of sadness and the tears that began to flow gave hope— hope that you can connect with the power that is found inside once you wake up from your 'mind sleep.'"

She smiled gently. "We are finished for today," she said in her calm but resonant voice. "Ask yourself which is more important; to hang on to the mental illusion of who you think you are, or to wake up and find the glory of God's creation: you."

Chapter Four

Time to Feel

The breeze, which had been picking up in intensity, whipping around leaves that had begun their autumn migration from the trees, slowed to a gentle calm. The last rays of the sun were falling behind the distant peaks of the mountain, and the sky gave a faint red glow as day finally turned into night.

Having placed my jacket on the ground, I moved sometime during the conversation with the old woman from the mountain to sit in front of the rock with my back resting against its smooth edge. She had been gone for some time now, although her presence lingered. I stayed to experience the nothingness of thought. A leaf gently brushed against my right cheek as if to say, "There is more than nothing; everything about life is surrounding you." For one of the first times, I just enjoyed being, knowing that I was one with the vibration of this peaceful mountain setting.

Tonight, I wondered, *will my mind resume its normal clutter— wondering about this, thinking about that?* It seemed that I was an expert at occupying my mind with thought and yet rarely thinking about anything that would help in answering the question the old woman had posed: "Who am I?"

I remember not long ago making my first drive across the mountain in many years. I knew that I was drawn to the mountains. Their age seemed to carry with it wisdom and comfort—a feeling that was seldom found in the hustle of more urban life. As if destined, perhaps a wake-up call, I had heard on the car sound system a song—a song I connected with years earlier. And as the song played, I could not control the tears which streamed from my face.

"I am, I said, to no one there, and no one heard at all, not even the chair. Leaving me lonely still." The song, recorded by Neil Diamond, had seemed to touch every fiber of my being. I recall hearing that song as a child and knowing that the words written and sung were somehow mine. That was exactly how I felt, lonely, crying out to be somebody, and no one was there to hear.

I hadn't had that feeling in years. But deep inside, I had recognized it instantly. It was as if I had lost control, the cap on the well of feelings had been removed, and, in the emptiness of the vehicle, I was free to experience just how alone I had become. Isolated by things, I was occupied with this and that, spinning the plates of life, masking the empty feelings with action.

"Who are you?" The question asked by the old woman from the mountain was profound. I was what I did—at least that is the answer that I would normally have given. Yet, if I was a salesman by trade, was that, in fact, who I was? If I played music, was I only a musician? Surely James Taylor is more than the songs he has written and performed. Surely Wayne Dyer is more than an author of many best-selling books. Surely we are more than what we do in our lives!

As I remembered the tears flowing, I felt a depth of loss, that years of life had been wasted, time spent in doing and not in being. Little did I realize that, once opened, the suppressed well of feelings would continue to surface, guiding me to answer the question asked. As the sunset faded, I decided to venture out, off the mountain, and gather with others. Perhaps in a different setting I could get a message that would help me when I saw the old woman again.

Going with no particular destination in mind, I followed my instinct but expected little from my walk. Perhaps it would be only another mindless exercise or a way to put my mind to work and escape the depth of feeling that I had experienced just hours before.

Off in the distance, I heard the sound of ancient drumming, and more than just sound, I could feel the vibration. My mind, once again, seemed to drift away from thought in the crisp night air. As if by impulse I was drawn to the pulsating rhythm that synchronized all who followed. The closer I moved to the sound, the more intense the vibration became.

As I rounded the corner, I became aware that many others were being drawn. Smiles, connection, dancing—it seemed that I was being surrounded by people who were *being,* and the sight was something to behold. Never had I seen this before. Scores of people were there contributing to the vibration of the moment. A drumming circle had formed, but it had become more. Almost as if this was the heartbeat of the city, people from everywhere had come to feel and be part of the vibration. The feeling of life was strong in that mountain town, but I had a hard time letting go—which was strongly characteristic of me.

"Who am I?" The question rang in my head. All around me were people moving, feeling the rhythm as they interpreted it, and none that I could see were being what they did. I watched as a little girl, blonde with a dress that looked like a princess gown, jumped between the rocks that formed this open-air park. Another older lady whirled and spun, oblivious to those around, as she had become one with the music. A young woman moved barefoot from side to side, jumping while her pants began to slide down. The picture was humorous; she would be forced to abandon her connection to the rhythm in order to pull up her pants.

Hundreds must have gathered, some playing along and becoming part of the heartbeat and others letting go of definitions and just being. I could not let go—not completely. I suppose my 'mind sleep' was too strong. For moments, I could close my eyes and lose track of who I thought I was, where I was and when it was, and just be. Then, I was sucked into my mind's activity, thinking about if I could 'let go' like so many of those around me. The very act of questioning was a clear indication of the mind's power over me. I wondered what was in me that prevented me from letting go.

As I sat there, perched against a rock, I noticed that there were two groups of people gathered. There were those who observed and those who participated. The people who participated—whether drumming or dancing—were far more present and seemed far more filled with joy than those of us who just watched. For a moment, I closed my eyes and felt. Could I trust my feelings and believe in being, or would I stay hidden beneath my trusty armor and observe as life passed me by?

When I opened my eyes, I noticed that most who watched seemed to have a sad desire in their eyes. Too connected to the wheel of business or of parenthood or whatever wheel defined them, none seemed to have the courage to step off and just be. I felt sad that I was in that group. For a few brief moments I thought I should join in the activity, but more than likely the problem was that I thought. Perhaps with time I would fully awaken from my "mind sleep" and truly "be."

Chapter Five

Night Vision

As I maneuvered my way to the top of the mountain, I felt something I hadn't felt for a long time—peace. In some ways, it was like the weight of the world had been lifted from my shoulders. No longer was I encumbered by the responsibilities of my "mind sleep" as the old woman had called it. Somehow, I was beginning to feel that maybe, just maybe, I could begin to learn who "me" really was.

When I breathed in, it was as if each molecule was infused with a freshness that would cleanse my body. As I stopped for a moment, it occurred to me that I hadn't noticed, much less felt, my breath for years. There was always too much going on to notice.

Tonight, however, was a special night. As I sat pondering all that I had been told, I began to realize that I was one with everything around me. Void of external light at the top of the mountain, the stars shined with a vivid clarity seldom, if ever, seen by city folk. Their beauty was hard to describe. Floating in what seemed to be a dark sea of night sky, I was looking at stars and galaxies so far away that my naked eye could see only the faint glow of light. And here I was, sitting, listening, seeing and feeling life in its many forms, just being.

Off in the distance, I heard creatures unrecognizable to me singing, calling out, and announcing their being. Without notice, a tiny lizard crawled across my foot, startling me out of my dreamlike state. There is nothing like an unexpected creature to change one's awareness. It drew me back into an awareness of where I was that very moment. Although, for the moment, I had lost the feeling of just being, it soon hit me that this tiny creature was part of just being. All he had done was remind me to feel and be aware.

In my head, I wondered what I would hear next from the old woman from the mountain. Her probing questions had somehow begun to chink away at the fearsome armor I had assembled over the years. Piece-by-piece, tiny bits of it began to fall away as I started to become aware of what I truly felt. But far too much was left to say that I was anywhere close to being done.

The chill of the night air began to deepen enough that I knew it was time to move to the comfort of the indoors. It was hard to move away from such beauty. My mind told me that I was sitting here all alone, and yet my heart felt connected to all that was around me. Moving, I feared, would break that connection. But I knew better, and the time of the evening and chill of the air pushed me to different surroundings.

Sitting inside in a grand chair, I became mesmerized by the fire in the great stone fireplace. Everything had its purpose, each doing exactly what it was set to do. Each rock, once scattered across the mountainside, was neatly placed into formation, together forming a hearth on which to rest my feet. And the flames danced to and fro, never occupying exactly the same space.

As my body began to remind me that late evening had arrived, I gently closed my eyes. The question entered my head. "Who are you?" I heard the old woman from the mountain say.

"I am Chuck Gallagher," I heard myself say aloud, but no one was there. My response jolted me as I opened my eyes, hearing the drip of water somewhere else in the room. I couldn't imagine having answered that way. I would have expected to say, "I am a VP of Sales. I am a CPA. I am a music director." Any of those, at different points in time in my life, would have been normal answers. Perhaps, though, it was time to understand that I am more than what I do to earn a living.

Closing my eyes once again—a bit concerned about what might be revealed this time—I heard the voice inside my head ask, "What does that mean?"

"What does what mean?" I instantly asked myself. Now, I could have understood this conversation if it had been with the old woman from the mountain, but now I was having a conversation with myself about myself, and I must admit, I was confused.

"You are not confused; only your mind is confused. Quit thinking and feel." The words were clear, but the task was more difficult than it appeared. After all, I was blessed by my thinking ability, but feeling was like having to learn to walk again after a traumatic accident.

"You were right earlier," the voice said. "You are Chuck Gallagher. You are here for a purpose. Perhaps it's time you got out of your own way and do what you came here to do!"

The question that instantly arose was, "And what did I come here to do?"

I felt that I should be having this conversation with the old woman. I suppose I felt that I needed her wisdom and guidance, but sitting there on the mountain I knew that she permeated every inch of this area. Perhaps she was the mountain.

"You don't need me to help you find your own answers," I heard her say. As before, it was as if her voice came from nowhere and everywhere at the same time. "We will be together soon. For now, find your own answers. You've had them all along."

Without a cloud in the sky, the night was growing cold quickly, and the fire began to dance less as time reduced the wood to embers. My eyes closing once again, I began to have visions in the night.

"You are here to enrich the lives of others," I heard. "Be guided by that truth, and the rest will take care of itself." And with that, sleep took over my body, and I drifted away with a calmness that I hadn't felt in years.

Chapter Six

Morning Revelation

As if everything was operating on a natural rhythm, waking moments crept in after a restful night. All was still. Alone in the simple room at the top of the mountain, I noticed the calmness of my surroundings. There was no tension or stress in all that was around me. The leaves outside stood still as if to gently rest, awaiting the breeze that soon, too, would awaken.

As I rubbed the inner part of my eye, I felt a gentle touch on my right shoulder. Any other time, this would have startled me, but I knew it was her—the old woman from the mountain. Her presence seemed to belong, and, if truth were known, I was hoping I would see her soon.

"Have you any insights?"

She asked the question with that now-familiar voice that seemed to bring calm and assurance. Her grey hair gently flowed cross her shoulder as she turned her head slowly to the left to look at me.

I felt her look. Most of the time, when someone looked at me, I would see their look, but this look from the old woman was more than a passing glance. It was as if she looked into my soul. She could see beyond the exterior and connect with something deeper. Suddenly, though, noises rattled the silence, and I lost the feeling of her glance.

"Soon, those will not bother you." Her comment was unexpected. Once again, it was as if she was reading my mind. It was something that I was becoming accustomed to.

Without her uttering a word audibly, I heard once again, this time through my being, "Have you any insights?" I had known that it was possible to know someone else's thoughts or begin to feel how they felt, but rarely had I experienced the power that this seemingly benign old woman possessed.

Turning slightly to my right with my right forefinger at the base of my nose and my thumb holding up my chin, I looked to the chair where she now sat as if to consider what to say. My mind raced to find the words. After all, I should certainly have something profound to say after a night of contemplation.

As I began to speak she looked away from me and uttered, "I know. Look to your left. Move your attention away from this room. What do you see?"

I was not expecting this change of direction, as just moments earlier I had been trying to feel so that I could explain what insight I had gleaned from the short time we had together just the day before.

"There's plenty of time for that. For now, just experience what God has given you. What do you see?" Her words, while calming, seemed also to provide direction.

As I looked from the mountaintop across the horizon, I could see for forty miles or more. The ancient mountain peaks had been there for more lifetimes than I could comprehend. But this day, as if the tide had come in, a sea of floating clouds encased the peaks, gently caressing what lay below.

"It seems that we are alone, in another world. How beautiful." I could scarcely begin to describe how awesome the cloud flow was as it embraced the mountains, leaving only the highest points to reach to the sun. In all the world, I wondered, just how many of us on this diverse planet would ever have the chance to witness such beauty and grandeur?

"There is grandeur in everything if you are awakened to see."

It was becoming clear that my thoughts were not my own. Perhaps I didn't want them to be. I rather enjoyed the old woman from the mountain talking to me before I had a chance to verbalize my thoughts. In some ways, it was easier that way, I didn't have to think so much. And just as soon as that thought appeared, I heard her familiar voice.

"That's the idea. Don't think so much. Experience *being* and all that surrounds you. Become one with the vibration of life, and soon you'll find that feeling becomes easier than thinking."

"Look out again," she continued, "What do you see? It is as if the clouds are the oceans and all that we see is all that is. Yet, we both know that there is more beneath the cloud cover than what appears above. Just like an iceberg only reveals just part of its majesty, so too, what you see reveals only a small part of the mountain."

"My question yesterday, 'who are you,' is best answered by what you see today. You are far more than what appears on the surface. Once the cloud cover of your 'mind sleep' is removed, you will begin to know the depth and breadth of who you really are."

And with those words, she stood to exit, leaving me with her final command, said in the gentlest voice: "Time to awaken, young one, and find out the majesty of what has been covered for too long."

It was as if I were in a dream. Somehow time seemed to slow, and what I had asked for—for many years—was now manifested. In the stillness, I could feel my heart beat. I could not say that I was fully connected, for as I would begin to think that I was, I would become aware that I was thinking again.

Yet what she said rang so very true. The seed beneath the leaves under the snow hides the potential for a mighty oak tree. The clouds rolling in like high tide at the seashore hide the majesty of the mountain supporting the peak that rises above. What we see, in most cases, is only an illusion hiding the potential—the true being lies beneath the surface just waiting to be uncovered.

Chapter Seven

More than a Speck

The only way to describe it was a day full of majesty. As soon as our conversation had finished, at least for a time, things seemed to change. At first, I think my ego was puffed with pride. I felt engorged with self. I had come to cherish the words from the old woman from the mountain, and when she spoke I listened, as she seemed to reach the depths of my soul. So when I heard her say, "find the majesty," I began to wonder just what lay ahead and just how big "I" might be in the grand scheme.

As she left, for a time, it seemed that around every point and in every action there was some new truth or revelation. I would guess that I only scratched the surface with my awareness. Self-importance did not diminish immediately. Yet, as time unfolded, my awareness seemed to shift. It was as if I heard her comments with filters on. The "mind sleep" was still active.

We have all gone through the experience but few, if any, remember what it was like—the details, I mean. Every child comes into this world with an empty slate. Our DNA infuses us with functions that tell our brain what to do to keep us safe, but beyond that everything that we see, hear and experience from conception forward is somehow written on that magnificent computer we call a brain. We are programmed to become aware of who we are, our surroundings and where we fit in this life. The fascinating part is that, once we become aware, we can never go back to unawareness. Deep within the recesses of our mind, we will always know. And the deepest imprints recorded are those that are generated by the greatest feelings.

In some ways, it was magical—at least to me—and before the night was over, the experience had turned cosmic. In the span of less than twelve hours, I had come to experience the power of a speck and the awe of a universe. Perhaps, in her own way, the old woman from the mountain knew just how powerful this mountain energy was. You did not have to be educated to learn life lessons here.

For some reason, there was a vibrant feeling here. Flowers that should have been long gone by this time of year at this elevation were still standing erect, soaking in life force from the sun and giving back vibrant color to please the senses. In the distance loomed a majestic mountain. For millions of years this mountain had stood. It was not a new mountain, like the Rocky Mountains. (Of course, new and old is relative in mountain years.) Rather, this peak in the Great Smokey Mountains had been there long before man and had absorbed the wisdom of the ages.

"Who are we—really?" I asked myself, beginning to feel small and insignificant with all that I beheld around me. The oak tree standing before me had dug its roots deep into the mountain, anchoring it there. Perhaps it will live two hundred years or more. I, on the other hand, am just here for what to the tree and the mountain is just a season. I became confused.

"Time to awaken," she said. "Awaken, majesty." All of those words seemed to swirl in my mind. What was she expecting me to find, I wondered? Then it hit me—*I've been thinking again. Every time I think, it seems I disconnect from feeling—and yet feelings create the most powerful knowing.*

I closed my eyes. What did I feel?

The feeling was one of comfort, nurture, protection and love, as if I was being cradled in a mother's gentle loving arms, wrapped in a soft blanket of sheep's wool. What I had or didn't have did not change the feeling of love. Sitting there, I began to grasp that every time I exhaled, I fed the trees just ten feet away. And, as they exhaled oxygen, they fed me. Life force here was strong, and the longer I stayed, the more connected I became.

Just an hour or so before dinner, I noticed a place that faced west. In the distance lay layers and layers of mountain peaks and valleys covered with life. Those closest were a deep greenish blue. Beneath the canopy of foliage, there was life undetectable to the human eye. But just because it couldn't be seen didn't mean it wasn't there.

Beyond that range lay another and then another and yet another. They went on as far as the eye could see, a sea of peaks and valleys with the sun dropping in the sky, soon to disappear. I knew instinctively that I must return as the sun faded from the sky.

"Do you feel?" Once again, the old woman from the mountain appeared to ask another question.

"Yes, I think so."

"There is no thinking about feeling; you either feel or you don't. Now, once again, do you feel?" the old woman asked.

"Yes. I feel a chill in the air." My response seemed lame, but at the moment she asked her question that is exactly what I felt. That was what came out of my mouth.

"Excellent." She seemed to beam with joy. "You expressed exactly what you felt at that moment. Notice no thought, just your feeling. Excellent!"

As I turned back to look at the sun setting in the western sky, I felt love. Turning back to tell her, I noticed she was gone. She knew what I felt. There was no need to tell her. A woman of few words, she knew that staying would only defocus me from my feelings—which I was now beginning to enjoy.

I focused inward, gazing as the sun crept slowly behind the mountain peaks. The large, bright circle in the western sky seemed to enlarge, growing into a giant orange ball slowly drifting downward.

Little by little, the color changed to a vibrant orange red until the last, smallest piece of the circle dropped from sight behind the farthest mountain peak, leaving a faint glow of purple and orange to follow into darkness.

Here I was a part of the life force I felt and observed around me. Some might describe me as a speck contrasted against what I had just witnessed, and yet I felt a power within that was far more than I have been willing to be. Perhaps I was discovering the answer to the question, "Who am I?" Then, as time passed, the night lesson was capped off with a stunning beauty far greater than I could have ever imagined.

Gazing into the night sky atop the mountain was breathtaking. There were no lights to distract the vision of the heavens. It was only the few of us gathered, the mountain we shared and a rich night sky filled with creation in motion—filled with life.

I became sad for a moment. This was the first time in my life that I had become aware of the vastness of creation. Many living today and many who have gone before us have been able to look up at night and witness this majestic wonder. Yet today we are so deep in "mind sleep" that we can miss the obvious. I know I did, and as I looked up I became aware of just how much a speck I might be.

Then, as if to jolt me back to reality, the silence was broken by a man talking to several others. He began talking about how the heavens were mapped by one man who had a quest for more—Galileo. I listened while allowing my feelings and connection to what I saw above to rise. The feeling of contrasting a "speck" to "majesty" began to come into focus. Here was this man, just a man, whose questions changed the course of the world as we know it. Galileo was just like me—a speck, in one sense. Yet, through his life, he answered the question "Who am I?" and changed the world.

"Very good!"

I felt the old woman from the mountain speak, though I didn't see her in the darkness of the night. Perhaps she was not there at all, or perhaps she was everywhere. Either way, her presence felt good.

"Your journey is well underway. But it is not a destination you seek. Remain aware, and feel."

Her words faded into the night air, and I felt calm.

Chapter Eight

Time to Go Deeper

Much of the next day had passed when I heard her faint voice again. "Are you ready?" It seemed that her visits would come at the most unexpected of times, but I spent much of the day anticipating this very moment. Smiling, I felt a certain joy, almost glee, when the question came.

"I saw that. So you are feeling without me prodding, very good!"

Her words carried with them the gentle feeling of unconditional love. Whether real or in spirit, I knew that the old woman from the mountain cared deeply. If this had been her job, then I could only wish to have employees who had such heartfelt dedication. But, of course, I knew that this was far more than a job.

"Are you ready?" she again uttered. As her words came I noticed, for the first time in days, clouds forming in the sky.

The portion of the sky not hidden by the incoming clouds was bluer than a robin's egg. The sun beamed through the sky, shining rays of light which danced in the trees as they prepared to shed their leaves for the winter. It wasn't until that moment that I noticed a change in the air. The breeze that brushed across my cheek had an unusual edge about it. Change was coming. I could feel it.

"For what?" I replied to her earlier question.

"To go deeper!"

I knew from the power of her tone that today she meant business. Not that her questions were trite, but today—just like the change in the air—I felt that whatever was about to take place would be significant. *I'd better be ready!* I thought.

"Where are we going?" Thinking I'd be cute, I tried an old standby technique that worked like a charm most of the time—deflection.

"You know that won't work with me," she exclaimed, knowing full well that I was just trying to play with her. "What are you feeling right now?"

While I was sure she knew what I was feeling, I'm not sure I knew. For a moment I stopped. *What am I feeling,* I asked myself, hoping she would not be reading my mind. Then, breathing in a couple of times, I began to get it. I felt apprehension. I was not in control and had not been since we'd first met. What we had done so far I could handle, but going 'deeper' had me worried and fearful.

"What do you mean 'deeper?'" I asked half-heartedly, trying to deflect attention away from my feelings while actually wanting to know the answer. Either I could get the answer to my question or I could postpone where she obviously wanted us to go today. I had the strangest sensation that today's visit was not going to be a brief one.

"If you want to know who you are, then you've got to be willing to face the truth of where you've been. Where you've been and the choices you and others have made are what got you here today. As a choice is made, it is like throwing a pebble into a calm pond. The ripples that follow are the consequences of your choice. Your life experiences, for the most part, begin to define who you are. So I ask again—are you ready?"

"But what are we going...?"

"Enough of your mind games. I don't have time, and neither do you. Are you ready?"

This time, while I knew love was still there, I could hear a certain commanding urgency as it became abundantly clear that she was growing weary of my procrastination and deflection.

"Yes. I am." As I spoke those words, an acorn dropped from the massive oak tree that I had come to lean against, hitting me square on the crown of my head. Startled, I began to laugh, feeling inside that this was God's way of showing me that it was good that I had come to my senses. Things that I would otherwise have missed now seemed to be more real, more meaningful. It was as if 'feeling' somehow awakened my senses to the life and meaning happening all around me.

"Today, we will spend some time together—alone—in quiet. You will begin a process that won't end today. Rather, today will be a beginning. You will be changed, and you will change. You will come to understand the foundation of who you are, which will unfold in ways neither of us can begin to know. I am your guide through this process. It is not my process. It is your process. I am just here to support your efforts. Before you even knew me, you summoned me so I could help you. You said come, and I did. It is now time to begin. Let us sit."

With those words spoken, we both sank into a sitting position beneath the enormity of the oak tree. It was as if this was not the first time for this old mighty oak. I felt as if the vastly extended branches were there to protect me from what might be a pending storm—and not just the physical one approaching, but the psychological one which might be on the horizon. I felt confident the oak would weather the storm and would share its strength with me, and a calm assurance knowing that I could draw courage to heal what needed to be healed within me.

One thing I knew for sure: the old woman from the mountain had stirred emotional strings that I had thought had gone silent. I expected what was to come to be no different.

As if to confirm what she already knew, I heard her ask, "Are you ready?"

The answer—obvious—"Yes, I am ready!"

Chapter Nine

Looking Back

"Close your eyes. Breathe in deeply, and slowly release the life-giving air you have taken in." She spoke with a quiet calmness that was clearly different from the voice I had heard only minutes before when my mind was active.

It was mid-afternoon. The sky was clear blue with only a faint stretch of a wispy cloud making its presence known as if it had been drawn there just to show the contrast of color—white against blue. I was still, and as she talked me through breathing, I began to notice less of her and more of everything that surrounded me.

Off in the distance, I could hear a bird—no, several of them, chirping as if at a neighborhood party. Much closer, I could hear the rapid vibration of a bee's wings as he gathered the last of the pollen before winter arrived. The world melted—that would best describe how I was beginning to feel. It was as if I was melting into all that surrounded me, and there was no "me" separate from anything else.

"With your eyes closed, you feel something touching you. What is it?"

"A feather," I replied. While I don't know whether that was true or not, it was true to me. "It's downy feeling, but my sense is that it's from the underside of an eagle."

"Very good." At her words, it seemed that the feather was lifted by the faintest wisp of wind and carried away.

"You are the feather; the feather is you. Go with it and see where it takes you." As the sound of the words rang in my consciousness, I began to feel a sense of movement—flying—being carried to somewhere.

There was no sense of concern. I felt supported by the wind. As the wind rustled through the leaves soon to be released from the trees, I could almost detect someone's statement, "You are loved. I will support you." I can't say that I had ever been spoken to by the wind; in fact, in my full consciousness I am not sure I would have heard the message. But now, I not only heard the loving words spoken, but felt the support of their meaning.

There was a freedom to flying, and the view was magnificent. Above the treetops, through the branches, over the next knoll and into the valley below—the ride was awesome. The experience was like what a bird must sense when it opens its wings to fly—soaring as the wind supports its grandeur.

As we crested the knoll and moved into the valley, I noticed the wind begin to slow, allowing me, "the feather," to gently rest in the contour of a majestic rock that protruded from the earth below. At landing, I wobbled a bit, as if to see if this was the end of the journey, and then nestled into the comfort and support of the rock. No words were spoken; I just felt the words, "you are safe," coming from the vibration of the rock below.

"Where are you now?"

Her words did not startle me, as somehow I had always known she was there. Yet I did not see her. I could tell that I was nowhere near where I had started. I was in another time and another place. Not a place unfamiliar, but a place far different from the tree I had been perched next to just minutes ago.

"I am here," I replied. "I am on a rock in the majestic forest of my ancestors." As I spoke those words, it was not me—"the feather"—speaking, but me an eight-year-old Indian boy. I was sitting with my legs wrapped around the rock as I had done many times before. This had become my vantage point where I could see the vast mossy stream that etched its way through the mountain to the land below.

"I am a boy," I exclaimed. "We are here."

As those words sprang from my mouth, I felt her speak, "Yes, we are, and it is good. What is your name, little one?"

Her tone had changed. She seemed much younger in voice, and although I had to have known that she had been with me the whole time, she still asked me, allowing me to lead this journey.

"I am 'Little Feather.' I am called that by my father because he says that I run with the speed of the wind. Sometimes I think I can almost fly. One day I will be known as 'One Who Flies,' but for now I am 'Little Feather.'"

In her next words, it was as if the entire forest was speaking, "And do you know who you are?"

The wind rustled, the trees swayed, the rock vibrated, and all living things stopped as I replied. "I am called 'Little Feather.'" There was no hesitation, no wondering, no concern, just an exclamation that "I am!" And with that said, I felt proud to "be."

The dialogue had ended as I began to move from the rock. And, while I never uttered a word, I could feel my heart saying, "Come with me," as I began to run hopscotch down the stream bed on to my next journey. With every move of my feet gripping the smooth rocks beneath them, I lost awareness of the old woman from the mountain and became more fully present in the life that I was living. Just then, I lost my footing, missing the rock that I had clung to so many times before, and slid on the slippery mud that was beneath it, sliding on my rear at least half the length of a tree below.

While the words I heard were a language foreign to me, I felt the sting of "ouch" as I rubbed my now very wet backside, which had caught its fair share of rocks on the tumble. Then, without thought or control, I began to laugh. The feeling of joy emanating from the laughter was deeply satisfying. It was as if every living creature around could hear my joy. I was safe, as I knew I would be. How could I be anything but? I was one with everything.

As I looked up to the sky I could see the sunlight streaming through the trees, glistening and moving like a prism turning and being moved by every rustle of the leaves by the wind. I knew by the position of the ball of fire in the sky that it was time for me to return. My father, a great leader of our village, gave me the freedom to run—the freedom to "be." But I knew from his teaching that, while one may be given the freedom to roam, one also returns to where he is loved. With the unshakable foundation of the rock, I knew that I was loved. After all, I was "Little Feather."

Her voice, having been silent for a while, was heard again. "How do you know you are one with everything, Little Feather?"

"You will know soon enough," was my reply. "For now, let me enjoy being here once again. I love the feeling of this—my home." At that moment, I was there. There was no separation. I was not just dreaming, sitting under a tree and imagining this. For just those moments, I was reliving what I knew to be real, and I did not want that moment to end.

"Very well," the old woman from the mountain's voice resounded as if through everything near and far. She was one. She was part of everything that was around me. She was love, and I felt it. Soon we would go deeper. For now, I enjoyed everything that I was and the love that I felt from everything around me. It was bliss.

Chapter Ten

The Revelation

In the depth of the night, how can you tell where the sky begins and the earth stops?

As if by some form of magic, in the next instance we're again part of another time. In those moments, I lay on my back staring at the night sky—only this time I had advanced in age, perhaps mid to late teens.

The time of year was the same—fall—but the location was different. I sensed that for some reason we had migrated further into the mountains, perhaps to take advantage of greater richness from which we lived and grew. It still felt very much like home, but yet there was newness to the area that begged for exploration. The elevation and clearing where I lay exposed the dancing rays of light in the deep night sky in a way that I had never seen before.

The fireball of day had been gone for some time as the gleaming night ball had taken its place firmly in the clear night sky. There were no words like we have today to name the sun and moon, at least no words that anyone in this lifetime would understand or remember. That language had been all but lost, gone with the generations who knew better—the generations who saw no separation.

As I was lying on my back, I could tell life was teaming around me, only I could not see it. All I could see were the rays—specks of light—that seemed almost close enough to touch. Many times as a young boy

I would slip out into the deepest part of the night just to look above and behold. If I focused my eyes on just one of the millions of light specks, it was as if I was among those specks in the dark night sky.

The old wise one of the village, a shaman, told me I was one of those specks on the night of the full moon.

At least ten summers back, I remember sitting by the fire many nights in a row listening to him speak. "There is a Great Spirit who lives in all things. You may not see him, but he is there." As he spoke those words, I remember smoke beginning to swirl around his head as if to affirm his words as truth. Just being around him seemed magical at times.

"How do we know there is a Great Spirit?" I recall asking innocently. I did believe. I had always believed. I just wanted to hear him speak in wisdom. Sitting at his feet, with the fire crackling in the background, was mesmerizing to me.

He turned his head slightly to look at me, but stopped, glancing somewhere above my head as if he were talking to an older spirit. "You cannot see the wind. Yet when it caresses your face you can feel it. When the leaves rattle in the trees, you know it is the wind. And, Little Feather, when the eagle loses her feather, it is carried far and fast, just like you run, like the wind."

"You may not see the 'Great Spirit', but that does not mean he is not there. The Great Spirit is everywhere, in all things, at all times. He is in you as we sit and in me as I speak." The words of the old wise one of the village had become soft, reverent, as he spoke of the life force that binds us all.

His next words startled me as a young child. "I will not be among you long. Soon it will be my time to pass into all that is. But just as the Great Spirit lives in me, so he lives in you, and soon it will be your turn to share this mystery with others. That is the cycle of life, and that is your destiny."

"I am like the leaf on a tree. Soon I will fall—drop to the earth. My body, just like the fallen leaf, will be consumed by Mother Earth, and I will be reborn, just as the leaves on the trees will reappear six full moons from now."

"My words, spoken to you this night, will be spoken through you for generations to come, and I will sing as the wind as I am one with the 'Great Spirit.'"

At the time, there was much of what he said that I did not fully comprehend. Riddled with emotion, I did not want him to leave and did not fully understand he was speaking of death. When you are young, you don't fully grasp the circle of life and the reality of physical death.

I was dismissed after his last words were spoken. That was the way of the old wise one. He spoke, and when he was finished, it was time for those who heard to leave and ponder their meaning. As I walked away, I recall feeling empty, already missing the man I had grown to love and not fully understanding why.

Tonight, however, some ten summers later, I knew better what he had spoken of that night. He did fall. It was his time back then. And I, lying here, knew that he spoke words of truth.

Many times since, I had heard him speak, in the gentle babble of the brook, in the resounding thud as the branch of the tree gave way under the weight of new fallen snow, and mostly in the rustle of the leaves as the wind reminded me of our oneness. His simple fireside lessons had shaped me, and now I had become as my father had said, "One Who Flies."

"Thank you, 'One Who Flies.'" I had almost dismissed my company, the old woman from the mountain. But I never missed her presence. She was the warmth that cradled me in the night air, the cool water that cleansed my skin. She was all that was around me. She was the presence of love.

"It was not my speed that caused that name to be; rather, it was a vision I had of an eagle. I could see things that others could not."

"Tell me more," she asked, knowing already what I was about to say. Then again, her questions seemed to focus me on this path—this journey. I was here for a reason, and she knew, as did I, that it was a time of discovery—an awakening of sorts. It was my time.

"The shaman," I began, "gave me a gift from the 'Great Spirit.' He gave me the gift of his vision. When he said, 'My words, spoken to you this night, will be spoken through you for generations to come,' I have come to know that he spoke truth. It is my responsibility to help others—to speak words of hope."

"It is time to go. Your work here is done." As she spoke those words I felt a gentle rumble within the mountain and knew that my past life memory would soon be but a faded dream.

As I woke from what must have been a lazy afternoon nap there under the tree, the old woman from the mountain was nowhere to be seen.

Leaning against the mighty oak, I began to rise, standing to my feet, knowing it was time to go. I was not conscious of all that had taken place, and that was good. Something had changed. The hue of the sun setting in the western sky seemed more intense. The sounds of evening seemed to be sweeter. There was something different about my connection to all that surrounded me. I wondered what, but couldn't put my finger on it.

Chapter Eleven

Back to the Now

D ays had passed since my last time with the old woman from the
mountain. You might think that, after such a vibrant experience,
I would be teaming with joy. Quite the contrary; I found myself
lethargic, moving from day to day with a sense of sadness, feeling
alone. It was as if the person I had been was awakened in spirit so many
lifetimes past, but now, all I felt was discontentment and disconnection.
What had happened to the awakened one that I sensed was myself so
many generations before?

Moving from day to day, performing the daily tasks of living,
seemed to provide little joy. One thing seemed to call for another,
and soon it all became an endless circle of one task—then another—
none holding much purpose. "One Who Flies" had purpose. That
thought entered my head with leaving me feeling a twinge of jealousy
and wishing I had half the purpose he had as he looked up into that
night sky. Looking up in the night sky was meaningless for me as the
surrounding landscape lights and the smog of the city dimmed all but a
few of the brightest stars.

There were no bills to pay, no meetings to attend; there was only
the necessity of providing for the daily needs. *It was a simpler time,* I
thought to myself, knowing that my thoughts gave me the excuse
for inaction. If I could find a way to pardon myself for the dead

feeling inside, I could find some comfort in knowing that I was not responsible.

"You're not responsible?"

As I had left the mountain days ago, her words didn't seem to have the same resonance. As I heard them now, they seemed thinner, more treble, vibrating not through the mountain but rather echoing off the buildings nearby.

"Who gave you permission to believe that you are not responsible?" she asked again in a voice that had become all too familiar. "Have you fallen asleep again, and so soon?"

The sound of her voice began to reawaken the comforting feelings of love that were always present when the old woman from the mountain was near. Before speaking, knowing that she knew my heart, I had to admit to myself that I had drifted back into the sleep that, all too often, clouds the majesty of who we are. While on the mountain, and even a day or so later, I could feel it, but with each passing day the grind of modern day life robbed me of my joyful memory.

"Apparently, I have fallen asleep," I replied, "and I don't find it restful."

"No, I'm sure you don't. It is hard to find rest when your sleep robs you of your destiny."

Most of the time, her words were plain—her meaning clear. But this time, her last five words did not connect—"…robs you of your destiny." Early on, she had asked me, "Who are you?" Perhaps still I do not know. For a while I was "Little Feather" who became "One Who Flies." Knowing that, although it did not fully connect, made me feel good. Somehow, I knew that I was connected to that young Native American, but I am not he, and surely he could not be me. It was just a dream, a thought created out of thin air. Nonetheless, for that moment, when I was "One Who Flies," I was!

"You were? My, how little you have learned. We have much to do."

Our dynamic was becoming rather comical; I would think it, and she would respond. At first, we'd actually had conversations; now our conversations were thought transferences. Mind you, I was happy to have her around. Each time we were together, she brought more joy, and that was something that was sorely missing from modern-day life.

I had stopped from my journey on the busy sidewalk, standing still as if time had frozen. People were passing me, some to the left, others to the right. Occasionally, I would get an odd stare—a look as if to say, "What are you standing still here for, you moron? Should you be moving like the rest of us?" When I was with the old woman from the mountain, it seemed that time did not exist. Carrying on a conversation with someone that no one else could see—at least I didn't think they could—seemed perfectly normal. She chose the time; I just had to be present.

"What did you mean when you said, 'robs you of your destiny?'" I said out loud right there in the middle of the sidewalk. Two heads turned as I spoke to no one there. The look on one woman's face was priceless. It was as if I had grabbed her purse and asked her for a date—all at the same time. She jumped and picked up her pace, knowing that something had to be wrong with me. I couldn't help but enjoy the humor. When you stop and become fully present, life does bring joy. Even with the chaos surrounding me, there were joyful moments.

As if she had appeared through the maze of bustle that surrounded me, I saw a bright-eyed smile, the wrinkles of her aged face coming alive as she found joy in knowing that I could be present anywhere.

"Very good. You know you are loved."

One who rarely showed my emotions, I felt a rush of joy fill my soul. My eyes were welling up with joyful tears as I felt what she said and knew the truth of her words. Her physical presence was not necessary in order for me to feel the depth of love from this spirit guide.

"Remember 'Little Feather?' Remember what the old wise one of the village said to him?"

"I think so," I replied with a hint of hesitation, again to no one as I stood on the sidewalk, motionless. While it had only been days, perhaps a week since that encounter on the mountain, the memories etched in my mind were growing dim. I had a basic thought or memory, but the words did not readily come to me.

"It is important that you recall. There is a message there for you. Your destiny lies within. You have begun to awaken. Do not fall back asleep and miss your opportunity here in this lifetime. 'One Who Flies' did as he was instructed. You have been given the gift if only you awaken."

Stunned, I stood there, timeless, in the middle of a busy sidewalk, unaware of anything surrounding me. The clear mountain air seemed to touch my nose with freshness and caress my cheek with a renewed wisp of love. As clear as the sounds of the horns blowing—which were noiseless to my ears—was the sound of the babbling brook near where I'd sat that day on the mountain. Water trickled effortlessly between rocks as a golden leaf turned in circles in the small pond below. Soon, the leaf would turn once too often and would find its way floating downstream, following its destiny.

There, for that moment, I felt more alive than I had felt in days. As if jolted with energy, I knew in my heart that I could not fall asleep— at least not spiritually. Part of the mystery was unfolding. Her first question, one that I did not know or think to ask, was being revealed.

Just at that moment, I heard an unfamiliar sound—certainly unfamiliar in the city. A hawk flew overhead, screeching out its distinct call with its wings spread wide riding the current of the wind. It made no sense. I could not understand it. I was not even sure I believed it. But, with every ounce of my being, at that moment I knew, I was "One Who Flies." The hawk, out of place in this vast city, was my confirmation; above all sounds, his was the voice I heard.

Chapter Twelve

Finding the Meaning

"Your destiny lies within." Her words transfixed me as often they did. The old woman from the mountain had a way of penetrating her meaning to the core of my soul. "There is love in protection, and there is love in letting go." I have experienced both in my time, but the love I feel from the old woman seems unfathomably deep.

I heard the squeal of a little child being carefully watched by his mother as she kept him from the harm that could come from one simple wrong move in the unforgiving city. It was now, and I was here. I couldn't stand there on the sidewalk forever. I was not a mannequin, and destiny does require action. Mindlessly I walked, going nowhere, deep in thought.

There had been some change—I could feel it. From that first time crossing over the mountain I knew something was different. There was an inner longing there, not something I could describe, but something that seemed to gnaw at my soul. I had felt it when I was much younger, but then, just like "Little Feather," I'd been so caught up in the energy of youth that I had missed the deeper meaning that lay beneath.

Never in my wildest dreams would I have guessed that my life would be so radically changed. On the outside, I was the same. My friends would not, in this short time, recognize any difference. But I knew. A force I could not explain was drawing me to something I did not understand for a reason I did not comprehend.

Words like "connection" and "feeling" had not been part of my vocabulary in the past. I was a "thinker." I was proud I was a "thinker." Most of the time, I could out-think most of those around me, and it served me well—or at least so I had thought. But now I was coming to understand that every time I "thought," it seemed to get in the way of my awakening. Perhaps I was quick with a thought but, in retrospect, I found little joy or love in the thought exchanges. I was stirred deeply and felt a love that was unconditional when I opened up to feeling with the old woman from the mountain.

"Stop." The red hand was flashing at the city crosswalk reminding all who stood there that there is a time for everything, including the right time to cross the street. But I was again transfixed, deep in thought (which at times was dangerous).

Every time I connected, I was on the mountain, I thought, wondering when or how I could ever reconnect in order to recall or remember the message given to "Little Feather."

"Go tonight to the highest place you can find in the city. Go alone. Look into the night sky. You do not need the mountain to connect with who you are!"

While I never expected them or knew when they would come, the answers she gave were always welcome. It was best for me to accept what I heard. My thoughts of who she was and how this was happening would only clutter the reality of what was, and for me that was what was most important.

Rich granite, from deep in the earth, adorned the lobby of the large bank building where I found myself just hours after her last comments. I had been here before, always aware of the sound of each person's footsteps as they walked across the opulent, artistic floor. This time, unlike other times before, I was with no one. It felt strange. Going alone to have dinner at the highest point I would have access to seemed dramatically out of character for me. But then, I was beginning to wonder just who this "character" was that was in my body.

Music, less than soothing, was playing as the elevator door opened to carry me to the sixty-third floor, my destination. Thump. Thump. Thump. By the time the door opened, I was starting to get a headache. Perhaps that techno beat was meant to energize, but I found it annoying. Once again, I was reminded how easy it was to become unfocused. It has been said that the one thing the ego hates is silence. If that is true, then we must truly be an egocentric society. Everywhere we turn there is some noise vying for our attention.

I was hopeful that the restaurant would be sparsely populated, as I was not sure how easy it would be to connect if mindless chatter was taking place around me. In fact, I was not sure that a connection was possible at all. The old woman from the mountain's instructions were clear. What was not clear was whether I was making the right choice by being here.

As I stepped into the restaurant entrance, a young woman stepped into view.

"Hi, my name is Sharon. I am your hostess this evening. Do you have reservations?"

I could not believe my eyes. Standing before me was one of the most beautiful women I had ever seen. Her skin was richly tanned with a look of fine silk—no imperfections. Her cheekbones stood pronounced on her face, and her eyes were a deep chestnut color that seemed to have a way of captivating the beholder. She was tall, well built, and healthy in appearance. But mostly what stood out was her jet-black hair, parted in the center and flowing smoothly across her proud, erect shoulders. She was clearly of some sort of Native American descent.

"One Who Flies" knew her. She was a member of his village. They had talked from time to time as she carried water from the stream. He knew that one day she would be his. He'd known that the first time he had laid eyes on her. But she would be no easy catch. Her name was "Raven Hawk."

"What am I thinking," I mumbled to myself, and there was a moment of awkward silence while she waited for my response. "Oh, I'm sorry. Yes. I do have reservations. You just looked like someone I knew years ago."

Her lips parted as she smiled as if to acknowledge awareness. Perhaps she, too, recognized me. Then thought crept in, and I shook my head. *This is now. She is here. Stay present,* I thought trying to push out of my mind what had seemed so real, if only for an instant.

"Follow me. I have a table for you with an awesome view. You look like you would like some time alone. Perhaps this table will serve you well. Enjoy!"

As she spoke those words, once again she smiled. Our eyes met, and I was absorbed in the radiant beauty of her chestnut orbs that seemed to look not only at me but also into me. Perhaps she was not the one I remembered, but her presence here was a sign. All was happening just as it should. *There are no accidents,* I heard myself feeling, and I knew it was so.

Looking across the night sky some sixty-three floors up gave a dramatically different perspective than one gets from the ground looking up. The only thing that disturbed the peace of the night air was the vision of air traffic as people moved about the country from one city to another. Other than that, there was nothing. On a clear dark night like tonight, the earth seemed to have vanished from view.

"What may I bring you to drink, sir?" my hostess asked, somewhat startling me as I found myself star gazing.

"Water would be fine. And, Miss, I don't need a menu. I'm eating light tonight. Could you just bring me a garden salad? Your house dressing will be fine. I just need something light. Tonight, I need some time to think."

She gently smiled and nodded her head, and after my food was delivered I never saw her again.

I suppose I had been sitting for nearly an hour when I found myself drifting as if into the blackness of the night sky. I am sure I remained in the restaurant, but at the time I did not feel like I was anywhere at all— or perhaps I was everywhere at the same instant. Whatever the reality, I had an eagle's eye view of the mountain and the territory we called home.

Transported back to that Indian village, I could see everything. I could see, but not as if I was there. This vantage point was different than in my first encounter. I was not in the village, but rather I saw things as a bird looking down—seeing as an observer, not a participant. I could see the strength and resolve of "One Who Flies." He was soon to take up his position within the council of leaders. He was chosen many moons ago by the old wise one of the village to speak the truth.

"Just as the Great Spirit lives in me, so he lives in you, and soon it will be your turn to share this mystery with others. That is the cycle of life, and that is your destiny." The words spoken by the mystical shaman seemed destined to come to pass as "One Who Flies" grew in his awareness of "the one."

There was only one last step for One Who Flies before he would take the old shaman's place. He must retreat into the silence, a sequestered Native American ritual that few had the courage or desire to undertake. It would be here that the circle would be complete. What had been translated so many years earlier would be transformed. Translation would become transformation, and the circle of life would be whole.

Somehow, as I sat looking out of the window in front of me, I knew all of this, oblivious to anything going on around me. My body was there. I was somewhere else, and I could see all.

It was the time when winter gives way to spring that One Who Flies left his village, carrying with him only an animal skin for warmth and a knife for hunting and protection. According to the village elders, he was the first to leave in over thirty-four winters for this pilgrimage into the silence. As he left, it was tradition that he must go as far as he could to a place where he had never been before. Two full moons must pass before he could find his place of solace.

It was a strange feeling, as I could see all from my bird-like vantage point. There was no sensation of time. Days or weeks seemed to jump like moments. One Who Flies would be here in my eyes, then there, until, at last, he found his place of quiet contemplation.

Having crossed over three mountain crests, One Who Flies nestled into a hillside area just below the frost line on the great mountain far from his village. This was virgin territory for One Who Flies, and as best he could tell, no member of his village or any other had been in this place for over two hundred winters.

Life was abundant in all forms. The last of the winter snows was beginning to melt as each day the frost line inched further up the mountain. Water trickled down in plentiful supply, nourishing the buds as life began to bloom again. Animals who had stored up for the winter were moving about, each in perfect harmony with the other. There was balance.

Present each day, One Who Flies called out a mantra that at first I did not grasp, but as time did not exist, the repetition began to etch the simple words into my awareness. Perhaps the message I was to receive was here.

"I am one within all."
"I am all within one."

"I am one within all."
"I am all within one."

"I am one within all."
"I am all within one."

The hostess' presence startled me back to the now. "I'll need to bring your check, sir. We are closing in five minutes." With those words, she turned and walked away, soon to free up the table that was the only thing standing between her and freedom from her evening work shift.

Oblivious to time, I looked at my watch only to discover that I had been sitting there for well over four hours. My trance-like state must have been the talk of the kitchen and wait staff. Rarely would they have someone barely touch their salad and yet sit motionless for such a long period of time. You would think at least I would have had to go to the bathroom. *Bet the boys in the back were taking bets on just how long I could hold it*, I thought as I excused myself from the table.

As I approached the lobby area, I could see there was no one near the elevator.

"I hope your time tonight was productive."

Her words had a rich, throaty tenor that exuded warmth and caring. I was surprised; I had not thought I would see that luminous black-haired beauty again.

"Thank you for your attention to my location. It was perfect."

"You're welcome," was her reply as, once again, I saw a gentle understanding in her simple smile.

"May I ask, how did you know I was in a contemplative mood? I mean, you had the table selected before I arrived." Not only was I interested in her answer to my question, but somehow I wanted to keep the conversation going. There was something that I could not put my finger on, a familiarity of sorts. Never had I felt such a knowing.

"Tonight was your night. I was told you would come. It came to me carried on the light touch of the wind. I'm sorry, enough of this talk. At times I speak what my heart sings. Sorry; I just had that table available, that's all."

Her last words were not from her heart. She told me what she thought I might understand. Yet I more clearly understood the meaning in the words that came from deep within.

Pressing for just another moment, I looked into the rich chestnut eyes of this messenger of sorts. "At times, my mind fails me. Your name again?"

"Sharon, to most." Then, as she turned, her hair falling off her shoulders with a slight glimmer in her eye, she replied, "But my friends call me 'Raven.'"

Ding.

The door to the elevator announced its opening, and with that jolt of unexpected sound, this dark-haired messenger from my past turned and disappeared into the hallway, never to be seen again.

Chapter Thirteen

A Greater Awakening

"I am one within all. I am all within one."

As I stood in the shower, my back to the water, I lifted my washcloth to my face just below my nose and breathed deeply, feeling the humidity surrounding me. With eyes closed, the hot water streaming across my shoulders with the vibrancy of a summer rain, I found I could not get those words off my mind. They seemed to permeate my being. It was as if I was not here, not there, but everywhere at once, and time stopped.

Standing for I don't know how long, I heard the old woman's rich familiar voice speaking, "There is more to be revealed. It is good. You are awakening from your 'mind sleep.' You soon will find the messages will come faster. Be open to what you receive."

As I reached forward to turn the water off, I mused to myself, *How can I not be open? A hawk soaring out of place in the city sky yesterday and lovely Raven last night; I think I am getting the picture.*

As connected as I seemed to have become, it was only for moments at a time. I still felt the separateness of myself from Spirit that surrounded me. Disconnecting from Spirit seemed natural, if not normal. I had the sense of "me," and I knew from my experience that I was not, for example, "that mindless moron who was driving at the speed of a slow turtle" in front of me. In fact, that judgment was part of what kept me in my "mind sleep," creating a difference between me and them. The words uttered by One Who Flies was quite different.

Fully caught up in the tasks of life, I soon forgot the tranquil experience I'd had in the shower just an hour or so earlier. Consuming my last sip of tea, I made way back to the car, completing the journey to a new church, visiting for the first time on a crisp, early fall morning.

As I walked toward the entrance, I heard the sound of music coming from within. Ever since I was a child, I have found myself transformed and transfixed by music (well, that is, most music; the elevator last evening was a notable exception). But in this case, I heard the sounds of strings playing, and I stopped, motionless as I heard and seemingly watched the sounds of heaven.

Moving his head forward and then back, this man was one with his instrument, and the sound he played came from the heavens. His long grey hair was pulled back into a ponytail with only a wisp dangling across his forehead. His skin was the color of the rich earth, and his look gave pause that he was familiar with the Mother Earth spirit within. As he played, his eyes closed, his fingers moving with seamless motion as if all of him was one with the instrument he played. The music was being channeled from the ethers; he was just the instrument to manifest the sound here on earth.

People, who walked into the building chattering to one another in conversation about whatever was going on in their lives, quickly stopped as his music seemed to have a healing, meditative effect. I could not help but wonder what message was there for me.

The place was a sanctuary of comfort surrounded by the chaos of daily life. Not that life stopped—it did not—but there, if only for but a moment, the energy seemed to change into a feeling that easily could be felt in quiet solitude on the mountain.

Funny how things happen unexpectedly. The one chosen to lead in music—not the one who was playing before the service began, but another—asked those gathered to sing "number eleven." Now I didn't quite get his reference at first. But quickly I observed a kind lady sitting to my right look at a collection of papers that we had been handed and noticed that these were words to songs. Number eleven was the song selected for us to sing.

The folks gathered began to sing. I turned in the booklet provided in order to join in. Others had begun when I heard these words.

"I am abundant."

"I am beautiful."

"I am kindness."

"I am love."

"I am creativity."

"I am expansive."

"I am receptive."

"I am one."

"I am one within all."

"I am all within one."

As the last words were sung, I felt it happening again. Confirmation was given. These were the words of One Who Flies. They were the words he had spoken over and over again during his time in the silence of the wilderness. There, during that time, he could contact the inner spirit unencumbered by emotion or mental confusion. He could complete the process spoken of when he had been known as Little Feather.

I remembered little of what was said following the song. My mind raced with one thought being replaced by another. *How could this be coincidence? Why me?* The old woman from the mountain said I was in "mind sleep." I would have re-characterized it as "mind chatter," incessant noise that blotted out the message that was desperately trying to make its way through.

I am. These must be the two most powerful words in the world, I thought to myself. Yet I found myself struggling between the inner recognition that "I am" and the conscious belief that "I am not." A transformation was taking place, but there was still something missing. My thoughts centered on my connectedness to others, and I began to notice in subtle ways the feeling that I was to be a messenger. *Perhaps that is ego speaking,* I felt as I refocused on what was being said around me.

"Refocus and listen. Remain aware. There's a message for you here." Those words written here were felt like a wave whose center emanated from my heart.

As the service drew to a close, a final prayer seemed to connect with me, as my mind seemed to still.

"May our inner vision open to the reality and the glory of the world of Spirit which is all about us; and to the companionship of loved ones in spirit who are here to guide us. May we be open to claim our destiny in spirit and in love."

Chapter Fourteen

Time Away

Two weeks had passed without a word from the old woman on the mountain. Then, as early morning sleep began to fade, I noticed that I had an itch on the very bottom of my right foot. I tried to satisfy the itch in my morning sleep state, but nothing seemed to take it away. I scratched against the sheet. No satisfaction. Then I scratched with my other foot, and it just would not quit. Then I noticed I had an itch on my left shoulder. Reaching around to scratch that area, I couldn't seem to get satisfaction there either.

What's up with all this itching? I thought to myself, still lingering in a half-asleep, half-awake dream state.

You know how it is early in the morning when you are starting to drift back into the world of consciousness while still connected to the world of dream. You seem to be connected in a semi-conscious way. It was then that the message came through.

"I've been trying to get your attention."

Still nestled in the comfort of my bed, neatly wrapped in my warm bed covers, I understood why my body had seemed to be calling and yet unsatisfied by various itches. I had so removed myself from my connectedness to the old woman from the mountain that these were ways for her to physically remind me or get my attention. It was time to return.

"It is time we continued," she said with a soft voice as I still lay sleeping, not sure if I was in this world or the next. "You need to know more. What you know up to this point you have managed to rationalize and put into your thinking head, but that's not enough. Every time you start to join the physical world, you seem to drift away from the spiritual. Until you can live in both, you will be challenged in accomplishing your destiny."

As I heard those words, thinking perhaps that I was dreaming, I noticed the itches had gone away. Had I drifted back into a mindless 'mind sleep' that easily?

The physical side of me wanted to stay in the bed and drift back into the world of sleep—knowing that I would forget what had just happened, knowing that I would stay firmly planted in the comfort of my 'mind sleep'. But I also knew instinctively that if I didn't listen this time, another would follow. Deep within, I wanted the message that the old woman brought, and deep within I knew she'd find a way to bring it. She was crafty in those ways.

As I got up to the crackling of a small fire in my room, I knew that I needed to take some time to receive. If I dared step back into what I considered "reality," I would miss this opportunity. I was caught up in the illusion of separation. Somehow I knew, or at least believed, that what I did every day, what I would call the reality of living, was disconnected from the world of Spirit.

We get up in the morning and begin to prepare ourselves for the day—both mentally and physically, but most of our effort goes into the physical. The actions we take are, in many ways, mindless. If you work away from your home, you get in your vehicle and make your way to work. You don't generally have to think about it; you just go. On your way, you tend to fill you head with noise. Perhaps you listen to the radio, finding out about traffic or hearing chatter about some company that is failing or some politician who wants your vote—mindless noise. You stop to get your morning coffee or other drink from the facility you normally visit. Do you notice who is there and make contact—real contact? Or do you find yourself placing the order, paying and drifting in and out of your thoughts, mindless to the others who are around you?

You get to work and begin the daily tasks at hand. E-mails need to be answered; they have piled up all night. You receive the first of many phone calls, each person needing your attention, seeking your help, asking your advice, wanting something. You move from one task to another, in many cases not thinking about anything that connects to the fabric of true reality. One task moves seamlessly to another until you find yourself noticing that the day has passed and it is again time to go to your home.

The disconnection doesn't stop, however, when work ends. You retrace your route, doing the same thing in reverse—listening to the same station with the same words that ring in your ears with meaningless information. "There's a wreck on this highway; traffic will be slow. You may want to take an alternate route." The words change; their effect is the same—disconnection.

When you arrive home, the scene is somewhat different, but not much. If you are married, you will hopefully greet your spouse with fond affection, but do you really feel the connection—really? Or is it more going through the motions? Pleasantries are exchanged, moving quickly to, "How was your day?" "What are we having for dinner?" "I've got to take the kids to gymnastics practice." "Sure, see ya later." And then the television is turned on so that all the pressures of the day can melt into another 'mindlessism' that keeps us from ever really connecting. All of this is keeping us caught in the 'illusion of separation'.

"Well, it seems those little 'itches' did get your attention."

The old woman from the mountain had returned, and her words were spiced with a little humor.

"Glad we've reconnected again. I've kind of wondered where you were." Just as those words parted my lips, I could feel her response shared with a straight love and honesty that I knew to be true.

"I never left," she said. "You just drifted away. You have a tendency to do that, you know?"

What she said, I knew to be true. I could so easily get caught up in my head that I would forget that deep inside I had a heart—which could feel. Without saying a word, I wondered to myself why I so easily left the world of feelings. I could honestly say the world of feeling—that feeling experience—was much more powerful than my comfortable "mind sleep." Yet, for whatever reason, I naturally opted to disconnect and stay in my head.

"You have the answer to that question, you know! Your asking is but another illusion your mind is playing on you. It is trying hard to force you to stay there—in your head. But, my child…"

That was the first time she referred to me as "my child." That caught my attention. My focus shifted. Was there a deeper connection to this woman who came into and out of my life at will?

"Don't get caught up in words," I heard her say with a more forceful voice. "Your mind is fighting for control. I have stayed away on purpose in order to give you time, to see how far you've progressed and where we need to go from here.

"You know," she continued with a more compassionate tone, "you can never go back. You have come too far. That's the reason you were compelled this morning to satisfy that 'itch' by getting up and visiting once again with me.

"Hear my words. No—feel my words. Once you have begun this journey, you can never turn back. You know what it is like to feel. You have felt the love of your homeland as you crossed over the mountain. You have felt the warmth and embrace of love as you took the time to just be. You have sat alone and felt tears of joy as you knew that in everything and everywhere love surrounded you. You have been changed, and once a change takes place, you will never be able to return to an unchanged place."

As those words filtered through my ears, they touched my heart. I do remember, for no reason at all, sitting still on the mountain and feeling a connection to all that was around me. I was surprised when tears streamed down my face at the memory. My conscious mind didn't understand, as there was nothing to precipitate my feeling, but my heart felt a depth of love that I could only describe as what a mother might feel for the newborn she just delivered—true, unconditional love.

"You are experiencing a state of emotional healing, and that is good. It is time for you to know more about One Who Flies and his experience. You and he are connected. Are you ready for more?"

Chapter Fifteen

Into the Wilderness

As she spoke those words to me—"Are you ready for more?"—I heard One Who Flies chanting, "I am one within all. I am all within one," over and over.

The vision was crystal clear. It was as if I had a bird's-eye view perched high up on a branch in a tall tree overlooking where One Who Flies had chosen to camp for the night. The fire was blazing. Its flames, blue at the base, turned into bright orange as they danced, some reaching several feet as best I could tell from my vantage point. From time to time, sparks would fly up lightly as if to say, "I can reach for the sky, too."

High above, there were no clouds, just a blanket of stars that seemed to reach straight down to the warm earth below. One Who Flies was wise for his years. He had chosen a place near a stream. It connected him to water but with an opening in the canopy of trees that surrounded him so that he could drift his consciousness away from the earth and soar to the sky uninhibited. His blaze kept him warm. He had surrounded himself with the four elements: earth, air, water and fire. Whatever was to take place was powerful, that I could feel, as One Who Flies had securely anchored himself to all the powers of God expressed in physical form.

Over and over, those words seemed to captivate my mind as they slowly began to sink into my being, "I am one within all. I am all within one."

I was not there yet. I did not fully connect to the meaning of the words. What I did know was that there was an emotional connection between One Who Flies and me and that somehow I was to learn from him. He seemed to have a direct link to all that surrounded him that was natural to him. From time to time, I had the hint of such a feeling, but those moments were rare. One Who Flies seemed connected always.

I felt anticipation. I was excited to learn; yet like starting any venture that is new and uncharted, I had a feeling of apprehension. The one thing I did have supreme faith in was the nurturing and loving feeling that the old woman from the mountain gave me. I knew that whatever lay ahead, it would be good or, maybe should I say, for my good.

"It is time for you to be still," the old woman said with an ever-softer voice. "You are there with One Who Flies—there in spirit, there in reality. Observe. Observe what you feel. Disconnect from this reality and join in his. He has much to teach you."

As her words faded, his seem to amplify. The sounds of the night surrounding me were just as real as those I had heard at the beginning of this journey when I sat outside alone. It was as if God's voice could be heard in the whispering of the trees. The old woman's words seemed to still my mind, and my senses seemed to come alive as my heart opened.

Perched above and looking below, I noticed that One Who Flies had begun to slow in what must have been his ritual dance around the fire. The night air was clear and crisp, and the fire put off an appealing aroma that seduced the senses. One Who Flies took his place by the fire, legs crossed and arms stretched with open palms to his sides. His words changed from his chant to more of a sacred appeal.

"Let us commune with the spirits of the air and fire, with the spirits of the water and earth." It was clear that the place he had chosen was special. This place, this night, seemed to open the door to spirit in each of these essential elements.

He continued speaking into the night for no one to hear. "Every part of me is infused with the light of your being, oh Great Spirit. I am warmed by the fire at night and the Sun by day. Fire gives me warmth through which I live and Sun the energy that sustains my life."

"The air, though invisible to my eyes, is carried by the wind and rustles the trees, making itself known. The air fills my lungs, cools my skin and brings fresh scent to my nose. With every breath, my life is refreshed by the air around me."

"As I dip my hand into the rushing stream, I feel the cool refreshing sensation of the water which flows past me. Touched to my face, the water invigorates my senses as it flows into my mouth and body. With each sip, I am nourished and purified from the inside out."

"Oh Great Spirit, I now sit here on the earth foundation you have provided. From it, I am sustained. From the animals that roam free to the plants that are rooted in its very foundation, the earth gives me the foundation on which I live."

"I am one within all. I am all within one."

Looking down in silence, I was transfixed by his words—the clarity of his thought, the truth of his prayer. I, who was so caught up in the physical, had missed the obvious. We cannot live on the physical plane without the air or water or sun or earth. Each of the four elements, while seeming so basic, also seems so often overlooked. But it is more than that. One Who Flies knew something and kept it foremost in his thoughts. We cannot live without the elements; those elements are a part of our very being—they are all within.

As those thoughts began to register in my consciousness, I heard the old woman from the mountain rise again.

"You need to stay here for the night and observe. As he receives his initiation, One Who Flies will connect with his great truth. He wants you to be here. That's why he called me to you."

"But why me? I don't understand what I have to do with any of this."

"Clear your mind. Your heart knows. You are here because you want to be. You are here because you are connected. You are here because you chose this path. You are here to receive a gift from One Who Flies. You are."

Her words fell silent, and as I looked down I saw One Who Flies lie down, nestled against the earth, as the fire grew dim in the dark night. What seemed like moments later, a shadow of his being rose from his body lying still on the ground. It was as if his spirit rose while his body slumbered. Translucent with a white blue glow, his spirit—I don't know what else to call it—seemed to move freely without effort, not constricted by time or space. I was still, like a bird perched high above, doing as I was told—observing.

Then, out of the shadows, another dark being appeared. It was the old wise one of the village who had left his earthly body many years before. Their combined translucent radiance seemed to illuminate in a mysterious way all that was around them. The trees seemed to reflect their glow with a new vibrant color, and the dying embers of the fire seemed infused with a rich red energy that I had never seen before. All that surrounded these spirit beings vibrated in a manner that acknowledged their presence.

"You have learned well. I see Little Feather has come far and now knows the mystery that we talked about so many moons past."

"It is good to see you again. I have seen you often in my dreams."

As One Who Flies spoke, I felt the love that bound those two vibrate in all directions, radiating a kind of warmth that felt comforting on a clear cool night.

"You spoke words to me, oh Great One, that I recall to this day." Without a pause, One Who Flies began to speak. "'The Great Spirit is everywhere, in all things at all times. He is in you as we sit and in me as I speak.' Those were the words you spoke to me as we sat by the fire."

For a moment there was silence. Not a word was spoken between them, although the words that I was hearing were, in truth, not being spoken at all. Rather, they were communicated as if by knowing through a heart connection.

"I heard you then," felt One Who Flies. "Now, I know the meaning of the words you spoke."

"Yes, it is your time, One Who Flies. It is your time to share, to help others come to know the truth. I am here for your initiation, for you now become the messenger, just as I spoke what to me seems just moments ago. Repeat these words as you feel them come from my heart to yours."

Before a word was uttered, there seemed to be a heightened sensation in the air around, as if every living thing was on edge. The trees stood still, not a leaf moving in the dead silence of the air. The night grew quiet. Tree frogs and creatures of the night grew silent as if waiting for the truth of the next moments. Even the remaining embers of the fire seemed to suspend their dancing glow. All hovered in anticipation.

"I am at ease in my body. I honor the natural world beneath, above and around me. Every need is supplied as I have faith in invisible reality."

As the old shaman closed his eyes and felt the words, One Who Flies enveloped them into his heart and, with no effort, radiated them out—repeated them as instructed—straight from his heart. The shaman continued.

"Through the air floats the power of my thoughts. How I think creates the experience that I have. My thoughts have power, and I surrender their power to the mind of my heart."

With each affirmation presented, absorbed and repeated, the translucent glow of the spirits below me seemed to increase with a glimmering beauty. I could not help but be warmed by the glow that was being created. Then, as if to acknowledge the increased power, the old shaman stepped back to give One Who Flies the space to radiate with his increased intensity.

His eyes closed, the shaman seemed to smile ever so slightly as he shared the next affirmation.

"Like the fire without, I am free to create, leaving the ties of the past that no longer serve. I burn bright with vision, turning hope into inspiration and inspiration into love."

With each affirmation, the anticipation seemed to build. I find it hard to describe. It was as if every hair on my arms was standing on end. The energy was reaching a critical stage, all seeming to wait for a final explosion—something that would change all that surrounded us.

Then, with the gentleness of a great grandfather looking with joyous love on his offspring, the last words were spoken and repeated.

"As the water carries sustenance, I nourish others with my feelings and imagination, trusting that my life is moving forward in keeping with the Great Plan of Spirit."

Without warning, there was a sound, an intense vibration that seemed to tingle through every fiber of my being. The sound was nothing I had heard before, almost as if every chord that could be struck was struck at the same time in perfect harmony and powerful resonance. The sound infused everything, both the physical and non-physical, and all the elements resounded in perfect harmony. All had become one. One Who Flies had become what he had chanted so many times before—all was in him and he was in all—perfect oneness.

"There is one more message I have for you," the shaman spoke. "Your message of light must go beyond those in your tribe. You will infuse your being into all that surrounds you. The power you will share will go beyond any earthly action you take. The wave of light you will broadcast will be received by others you draw to you, and the message will go forth in ways yet to be seen."

Chapter Sixteen

Decoding the Message

Just as his last message was spoken, I began to feel a drifting back, away from the world of Spirit and back to the illusion of reality. I looked at the alarm clock over on the nightstand and saw that only minutes had passed. There I sat, warmed by the fire in my room, and all that I had experienced when rejoined with the old woman from the mountain, all that time observing as she had requested, had only taken a few minutes. It didn't seem real.

Her words were real. They resounded through my being as if she was right there beside me—even at that moment.

"Your heart knows. You are here because you want to be. You are here because you are connected. You are here because you chose this path. You are here to receive a gift from One Who Flies. You are."

More and more I began to feel the power of those two words—"I am." No longer did I seem to doubt the power of being. "I am." The words resonated within and seemed natural. If she asked today, "Who are you," I would respond, "I am."

But what of the gift from One Who Flies? Was the gift the incredible sensation I felt as I observed him go through his initiation into Spirit? Was the gift the powerful affirmations I had heard? There were so many experiences that I felt, including the explosion of creation when oneness had been achieved, that I could not begin to determine what gift I was meant to have received. Perhaps it was all of them.

The more pressing question that seared in my mind was what she had spoken: "You are here because you chose this path." What path, I wondered? There was no doubt that in a short time my thoughts had changed, and my feelings had been infused with energy and a power that I had never experienced before. But I could not discern a path. If there was one, it was not present in my conscious thoughts.

As I rose from my chair, I noticed the early morning fire—which I used to make my morning activities a bit more comfortable—begin to wane. It was time to prepare for the activities of the day ahead. *How blessed I am,* I began to think as I made my way to take my morning shower. *I could never have imagined that my conscious thoughts and inner feelings would have been stirred in such a powerful manner just a few short months ago. Whatever happens, there is a reason.* Those last thoughts were preceded by the handle of the shower being turned on. *Just right,* I thought to myself as I stepped into a nice hot shower.

As the shower washed over my body, bringing a warm pleasure that adds joy to most every morning, I again heard her voice. No longer did I need to see her; I just felt her presence, and it was good.

"Many people have, at times, the experience of feeling themselves part of infinite Spirit—feeling, if only for a fleeting moment, an embracing of Spirit surrounding and engulfing their human personality. You have felt that and more."

As her words continued, I felt as if I was bathed in love, like each drop of warm water that flowed over me was drenching me in love beyond any measure of my understanding. The feeling was pure bliss.

"The 'I AM' is unveiling through you. Be open to the messages that will come to you. Allow your heart to be open, to be aware, to breathe with love. You do not need to think; you need to 'be.' And know, my precious one, that everything that happens is happening for a reason. Be open and know that the path will unfold in ways more splendid than you can imagine."

Chapter Seventeen

The Passing of Time

Months passed since that time of intense feeling, that time of initiation for One Who Flies. How simple and easy it is to become caught up in the illusion of daily life, immersed in the belief that it is real. Waking up, we begin to deal with thoughts of the day: what we are to do, who we'll make contact with, simple, daily thoughts. Most go to work doing something that funds what we call life. As we immerse ourselves in our daily tasks, it seems that we remove ourselves from the truth of who we are.

"I am." I am what? I am what I do? I am a husband? I am a father? I am a speaker? I am a writer? Easily the list could continue, each statement defining a part of the whole, each statement defining my place in the illusion of daily life. Each "I am" statement is limiting, and the true "I am" is unlimited. That is hard to remember each day.

Knowing better, even as I write these words, there is a part of me that wants desperately to believe that what some call "the daily grind" is real. Yet, when I close my eyes and silently breathe, I know that the process we go through daily represents the mystery of the illusion. Sadly, I wonder just how many have those moments of awakening, which give us a glimpse, an understanding that there is more—much more!

In a plane flying miles above the earth, I find myself once again regaining the sensation of just being. In this experience, I am unencumbered by the daily activities that seem to invade most every moment on the ground. Time here seems to stand still, to provide quiet time—time to reconnect. Sitting here, I wonder if I'll hear her words again. The voice from the old woman was comforting—challenging at times, thought provoking, and always emotion filled. I found my experiences with her to be powerful times of awakening. There have been moments over the past several months when I have felt her presence, when the words she spoke resonated true throughout my being. But, I admit, I miss her voice.

"Allow your heart to be open, to be aware, and to breathe with love. You do not need to think; you need to be." As I sit in a state of reflection, those last words she spoke to me seem more powerful—even today. "You need to be."

"You need to be," she had said—four words that seem simple, yet were difficult to achieve. Work. Phone. Computer. Internet. They are all distracters and beckoners. I need all those tools now. Demands on your time seem to move you away from just being. When can you be here? Go pick up the kids. Microwave dinner. The list seems endless as we focus on the process of life and the tools we use to live. One Who Flies was not distracted in the ways we find ourselves living today. Yet the struggles faced by those in other times and other places were just as real to them as ours are to us today. I imagine, almost laughing, that if One Who Flies could enjoy the creature comforts of our life today, he would wonder why it would be so hard for us to connect. After all, food is in the fridge, we have a roof over our heads, and we are seldom too cold or too hot.

Those words she spoke the last time we were together in spirit now have a different meaning as I look back. The times when I felt closest to my true being were when I was most present—connected with another soul, just offering myself, just being. How simple it is to focus on becoming and lose the fact that what is important is just "being." Perhaps that is part of the lesson since we, the old woman and I, last talked. Her instruction was clear, but to some—and I'd put myself at the top of the list—it is hard to "be" when so much of life is spent on "becoming."

"What have I learned?" That question popped into my mind as my plane began its descent. My thoughts seemed to stop as I reflected on the question. My feelings were mixed. On one hand, I felt sadness, in that I seemed to have disconnected from the powerful and pervasive feelings of love that had swept over me during the observed initiation of One Who Flies. Yet, even as I witnessed and felt that experience, I also knew that it was a moment, and moments of bliss don't last forever. How can one enjoy the view from the top of a majestic mountain if there is not a valley below?

This life—the daily illusion we live—seems always to be in a state of change and constant contrast. To understand "highs," we must observe or experience "lows." Everything has an opposite—success and failure, hot and cold, wealth and poverty, joy and sorrow. Perhaps in this learning environment—Earth—we must come to know those differences so the power of our "being" will gain greater understanding and have maximum effect.

How easy it is for us to live our natural life on this earthly plane and never have the opportunity to realize just who we really are and how powerful our thoughts, experiences and intentions have on others and life itself.

Staring at the seat in front of me, I wondered if I had followed her direction well. There were moments when I was touched profoundly and at unexpected times. Perhaps then I was just being, open to the moving of Spirit, to the power of connecting. At other times, I found doors of opportunity seemed to magically open with little or no effort on my part. All I knew when those serendipitous moments happened was that I was open in the moment to realize that something special was happening. At other times, I had the very real sense that I was in the right place doing the right thing, but for what purpose? Well, that was a mystery.

A baby was crying many rows ahead of me, two women were talking about their grandchildren behind me, and the engines were continuing their drowning roar as we began our descent.

"It's all right. You're doing just fine." I can't begin to tell you the comfort I felt as I heard her words ringing through my ears once again.

It's been a long time, I uttered in my mind as once again the old woman from the mountain and I reconnected.

"We've never been apart."

Her voice was rich and calming, and as she spoke I felt the truth of her comments.

"You don't need me with you to do what you need to do. You have been doing it already. I am always with you. You should know that by now."

Deep inside, I knew it, just like a child knows its mother's love. But I have to admit, it was nice to hear her voice every now and then. Her words were soothing, yet I was perplexed by her comment: "You have been doing it already." After that time of being with One Who Flies, I felt as if I had done nothing. No longer did I feel the sheer joy of being in the moment, the elation of feeling "I am" with everything around me. If I didn't feel the same, how could I be "doing it," and what was "it" supposed to be?

As the pilot's voice came over the loudspeaker in the plane, "Flight attendants, prepare the cabin for arrival," I heard her voice once again. "There you go, back in your head again. You'll find that you'll know more and connect better when you relax and quit trying to figure it out."

I knew she was right. And just as soon as her words faded from my ears, I was jolted with another sensation, the sensation of touching down. As the plane lunged forward with engine thrusters propelling us to an acceptable taxiing speed, I knew that something must have been going correctly. The connection wasn't lost. Still, I found the present moment, people standing, moving forward, grabbing baggage, preparing to deplane and rushing to connect to their next flight, a bit annoying. Reality always seemed to get in the way of those far too few precious moments.

Chapter Eighteen

Our Connection

"We are connected, you know."

I was startled by the voice that I was hearing.

As I was lying in deep sleep, the night was quiet with a late winter chill in the air. I had gone to bed late that evening after spending time catching up on e-mail connections missed during the day. While I'd started out with just a blanket and sheet, as the early morning hours crept in, I instinctively reached for my cozy down comforter.

I was in the deepest part of sleep, that time when there is little if any recollection of dreams. Perhaps then there are no dreams as the level of sleep is too deep. Yet this night I heard his voice, a voice that rang with a richness that would make many a radio announcer envious. Full and vibrant yet calming, his words reverberated throughout my being as I was sound asleep.

"You know who I am, don't you?"

We had never spoken, yet there was no doubt in my mind who this night visitor was. "Yes. You are One Who Flies." No words were actually being spoken, yet it felt as if I was fully awake and carrying on a conversation with a close friend.

"Very good. I wasn't sure you'd recognize me, considering this is my first visit with you."

I could hear a simple smile in his voice, perhaps mixed with some relief. It felt as if he was glad to know that our first encounter wasn't awkward.

I could feel my response deep inside. "I am glad you are here. I feel like I've known you all my life, at least in some form."

I couldn't really begin to describe the feelings that I was experiencing. There was something very odd about what was taking place, something in the depth of knowing. It was almost as if I was talking to myself, like looking in a mirror and having a dialogue with me! I know that I was privileged to have observed One Who Flies since he was known early on as Little Feather. But that observation in no way would have given me the deep feeling of knowing that I was experiencing at this instant.

"Why are you here?" I spoke no words, yet my thoughts were transmitted clearly through space and time.

"There's plenty of time for that. I'll answer your questions in due time. For now, just connect with my presence. Through the power of our connection, you will learn much."

He was right. While deep in sleep, comfortable in my bed, curled up and cradled in warmth, I began to notice a subtle vibration, almost a very slow pulsation. It was as if there was a merging of our beings. He was becoming part of me and I part of him. Perhaps it was my limited awareness, but I suppose all this time I had observed disconnection. I was separate from everyone I saw. Yet at this moment, I felt—for what I suppose was the first time—what appeared to be the joining of two as one. With eyes closed in sleep, we seemed to connect as one. I began to see and have thoughts as if they were his, not mine.

It was like there were parallel experiences taking place. On one hand, I was very much asleep, nestled in the warmth of my bed, and on the other, I was becoming one with my newfound friend. I had heard that when one dreamed it might be real in another time or space, but never had I experienced anything quite this real.

"You know that you are a part of me?"

His question, or what I would call a statement question, startled me. Mind you, it did not change the depth of my sleep in those wee morning hours; let's say it just caught me off guard. This whole experience was new and unexpected and yet quite calming. I knew that I relished hearing from the old woman from the mountain, but the depth of feeling was different here. It was as if a part of me that I didn't know was missing was somehow found. I was beginning to feel complete.

"How?" I replied. "How are we connected?"

Then the answer came rushing in without the need for words to be spoken. What had been hidden became crystal clear. The questions that had plagued me, the missing pieces of the puzzle were beginning to come together.

"That's right. We are connected. I told you that you would learn much. Now is the time for all to be revealed."

Everything and everyone—we are all connected. We see separation, but it is only an illusion. The truth is that we are connected. But every so often there are those chosen in their time and their generation to be the message bearers. One Who Flies had been one of the chosen ones. Everything that had happened to him was preparing him for his life mission and task. There are no mistakes. Whether we like it or not, everything has a purpose. It is up to us to live our lives and to fulfill our purpose.

Little Feather became One Who Flies as his purpose among his people and others in his time was to share the message of connection. That was nothing new to me; the visions I had on the mountain and at other times had already shown that to be true. Yet none of those visions had prepared me for what was next to come.

That night, the night I had traveled up to the sixty-third floor to have dinner, was the night I met Sharon—the one who was also known as "Raven." There was something strikingly familiar about that young woman. We were connected, too, although at the time I just felt a tugging at my heart.

It was all starting to make sense. Questions not even thought of were being answered. Purpose was becoming manifest in practical ways unknown and unspoken. As the sunrise gives light to the day so that what is in the dark is brought to the light, so was this unexpected but welcomed experience.

One Who Flies, once finished with his initiation, had sought what his heart burned for: Raven Hawk. They shared a depth of love and connection that many in my time would envy. But as the wisdom of the old shaman had been passed to One Who Flies, the time had come to share the message of oneness beyond the confines of the village and of their people. One Who Flies had been the chosen one. He was the one who was destined to share the truth, to expand awareness, to help others grasp the true power of our connectedness. He was also to connect us with the power of our being—of our "I am."

Together, One Who Flies and Raven Hawk produced a family of three, two boys and a girl. True to his name, One Who Flies found no limits, no boundaries. He roamed the mountains of his ancestral home and explored far beyond those borders, taking the message of oneness with him.

Revered by his people, whether of his tribe or not, One Who Flies was known as a powerful shaman. His people accepted his message of connectedness. Whether above or below, whether of water, fire, air or the richness of earth, One Who Flies easily moved among men and through Spirit, fully connected to the vibration of his surroundings.

Native Americans for generations had a deep and rich abiding love for the land and the bountiful gifts that it provided. They saw the circle of life and knew, instinctively, their place in the connectedness of all living things. That, however, was not true for those who were new to the shores of this land. One Who Flies was sent to expand the awareness of those who were new to the land—the man whose skin was pale.

His voice once again rang clear, and I felt the presence of his connection in those wee morning hours. "As our souls continue to merge, there is knowledge that may startle you, but it is necessary for you to know all of who you are."

In the comfort of sleep, I felt peace as I observed One Who Flies and his family. There was love, comfort and joy there. All the children were embraced in the love of their parents. I couldn't quite imagine what might be revealed that would "startle" me. Yet somehow I suspected that One Who Flies was not one to exaggerate.

At times, One Who Flies would go on quests to seek others, both Native American and pale skinned alike. For some reason, he was comfortable walking among people of different skins and seemed to be accepted by all. He had a peace that provided calm to those who walked in his presence. They might not have known why, but within there was a feeling of acceptance and trust that brought safety to One Who Flies.

At other times his quests were to seek alone time. One Who Flies knew that his wisdom did not come from within his own being. He understood that the collective wisdom of the ages was found in all things and that taking time to reconnect was the source of his power. It was during one such meditation alone, deep in the mountains, that he had a profound revelation.

As dusk gave way to night, One Who Flies, deep in the serenity of the mountain, began to smoke on his pipe and meditate. Those times of connectedness often paved the way for a deep rich experience, which gave One Who Flies direction and focus for the next part of his journey. Expecting something subtle like a nudge, One Who Flies found himself in a vision for which he was unprepared.

In the clarity of the moonlit night, One Who Flies saw his village being invaded. Women and children were scattering here and there as men with horses stormed their peaceful village. There was chaos. Women rushed to protect their children, seeking refuge somewhere, anywhere. From a place of peace, the people of the village were unprepared for this attack. No one in his village knew why. Men and young boys stood valiantly trying to protect their loved ones and their way of life.

Their efforts were quickly extinguished. Lives were lost as the invaders left as quickly as they had arrived. Then, as if with, telescopic sight One Who Flies watched his daughter being swooped up by one of the invaders as they sped out of the village.

"She has your gift."

As the vision ended and One Who Flies jumped to his feet, hustling to leave his peaceful meditation to return to his people, he heard the voice from the old shaman.

Again, he heard, "She has your gift."

What does that mean? he thought to himself as he kicked dirt over the smoldering fire, extinguishing it. He knew that time was of the essence if he were to warn his people and save his family. He knew also that his visions often preceded reality. He'd never thought himself a fortuneteller; rather, he kept to himself the gift of vision that so long ago he had claimed.

"Everything has its time. You've done well. You should be proud."

As One Who Flies heard those words, he couldn't find sense in them. He was consumed with his desire to prevent what he had seen so vividly in his night vision. He wanted to hear the old shaman—but as often is the case with fear—his cord was then too tightly connected to the earth and his family to receive the words of Spirit.

He began to run with ever-increasing speed. He was far from home. Yet he knew the mountain well, and every moment that he ran became a moment closer to preventing what he feared the most.

"Know this: even as you run—and run you will—you have done well. Your daughter is part of her father and will pave the way for your mission to continue, whether you do or not."

As those words entered the mind and being of One Who Flies, he stopped. For a moment, in the stillness of the night, he allowed time to cease. He became one with all around him, and time was no more. It was then that he knew.

In life we have a purpose. We may not know consciously what that is, but there is a reason for our existence. At that moment, One

Who Flies saw his and found peace. Of course, that doesn't change our humanness. One Who Flies was certainly still human and would do whatever possible to protect his family. He turned and ran like the wind, fully prepared for what would follow.

Chapter Nineteen

The End or the Beginning

Accepting our humanness is often hard to do when we attempt to view our cosmic connectedness. We are born. That is a beginning. We die. That is the end. Or is it? Perhaps what we think is the end is really the beginning. Whatever the answer, the reality was that One Who Flies was experiencing his humanness.

With a full moon in the clear night sky, maneuvering a run through the woods at night was made easier. In some circumstances, his desperate travel would have been impossible until daybreak. But tonight, movement was more possible, although the light of day would offer greater opportunity to increase his speed.

As he ran barefoot through the underbrush, small limbs and branches reached out and slapped his face and arms, heightening his senses. He was alert to impending danger. He couldn't completely reconcile what the old Shaman had said. For a moment, it had made sense, but as the speed of his feet increased, the depth of understanding faded.

Only his toes and the balls of his feet made contact with the wooded blanket of earth beneath. His feet felt no pain, although in the light of day it would become clear that running in the dark had left its mark.

When faced with great loss, the power of human possibility rises. One Who Flies feared nothing from the woods he traveled so often.

They were part of the "I am." He had said many times, "I am one within all. I am all within one." If that was true, then how could harm befall him when his cause was noble?

Running through the woods, following a familiar path—one that he forged—seemed effortless. His body was filled with strength. It soon became like fluid motion, much like the wind moves through the ripened grain or gently bends the tall pine. There was no resistance— just forward motion in harmony with all that surrounded him.

In the flow of his mission, One Who Flies could not get out of his head the words the old Shaman had spoken as his night quest began: "Your daughter is part of her father and will pave the way for your mission to continue, whether you do or not."

By now, it was the wee hours of the morning—those hours when all becomes still and the quiet moisture of the morning dew settles on the resting trees and growth beneath. This was the time of day when the earth is kissed, the time when nature seems to be replenished as it prepares for the rising morning. It was also the time when One Who Flies could sense the progress he had made from his night journey. By standards we can understand, One Who Flies was within 15 miles of his village. The only thing he faced as an obstacle to slow him down was crossing the narrow gorge with the stream rushing beneath. He could avoid this hazard, but it would extend his journey another five to six miles and add several more hours before he would arrive. That was precious time he could not spare.

In years past, he had undertaken to bridge this gorge by placing a large fallen tree across its expanse. Everything has a purpose. Leaves falling from the trees provide a blanket to protect the new growth of spring. Likewise, the death of the tall sycamore that reached above the canopy of the forest was not in vain; it provided just what was needed to bridge the gap from one side of the majestic mountain to the other. And many times, more than he could count, One Who Flies had crossed that narrow walkway.

At first, his crossing many years earlier had been tenuous. He recalled from many years past how he would straddle the tree and shimmy his way across, observing the streambed beneath him. Like anyone doing something for the first time, One Who Flies discovered his way. Moving the tree to pave the way for a more efficient crossing was obvious, but gaining the courage and footing to make it a natural bridge took time. But time was something he'd had, and by this morning, as he approached the gorge, One Who Flies had no thought of the tree or the bridge or the gorge. His mind this morning was filled with concern for his family and his village. His mind was consumed with the vision he'd had just hours earlier.

Like a cat moving easily in the dark with stealth and cunning, One Who Flies was easily traversing the mountainside. Early morning light beginning to cross the mountain peaks provided little illumination to the forest below. Yet, as those flickers of light bounced off the treetops, One Who Flies knew that soon he would reach his destination. The only question was, would it be soon enough to prevent the clear and present danger that he had seen in his vision?

While he ran with the speed and instinct of an animal, he could not get out of his head the words he had heard the old Shaman speak. "Know this: even as you run—and run you will—you have done well. Your daughter is part of her father and will pave the way for your mission to continue, whether you do or not."

As those words resonated in his head, he approached the last obstacle that stood between him and his goal. Once he crossed the narrow gorge, the remainder of the path would be easy, especially with dawn beginning to illuminate the way.

His left foot was first to reach the sycamore bridge, which now had become well-worn from years of weather and much travel. In years past, the bark had provided a sort of rough traction that made shimmying across the tree less than comfortable to a young Native American brave. But over time, the bark gave way to the effects of weather and travel, becoming comfortable and smooth to the touch. One foot followed another.

The streambed below was teaming with the sounds of life. The stream was doing what it did day after day, year after year. Water rushed over the ancient rocks, which were uncovered, discovered and eventually weathered by the relentless movement of the stream. Rocks could change the course or even stop the stream, but over time the movement of water would take its toll and wear smooth even the most persistent rock. In the end, the persistence would carve valleys and forge the pathway for new earth to be explored. One Who Flies, in his own way, had done the same as he broke free from the bonds of his people and carved new territory and thoughts to be explored by people who were new to his world. He was the stream to them. He heard the stream below as he placed one foot before the other, crossing the footbridge he had created.

With no warning, his next step was his last.

Chapter Twenty

Facing Change

At times, we can see what lies before us as we experience life as a sequence of events with a reasonably predictable outcome or future. At other times, the next step literally can change the entire direction of life as we know and experience it. We don't see it coming. We are unprepared. We are thrust into change. The constant in both scenarios is the same: change. It isn't that change happens; it is how we deal with change and the choices that we make following change that create the beauty of the journey.

For One Who Flies, one step, foretold by the old Shaman, completed a task well done and set into motion the continuation of a process started long before One Who Flies took his earthly form. While he was not conscious of the choices that had set into motion the next part of his journey, he knew with that last slippery step what he had known all along. He knew. He had always known at some level. We all do.

A thin mossy growth had taken hold of the now slick sycamore. The bark, its skin, had long since withered away with the many changes of the season and the many times it had served as a foot bridge for animals of the forest and for One Who Flies. The death of one form of life often provides the fuel or foundation for the creation of yet another form of life to begin. On this day, both were true. Had it been later in the morning when the dew-covered footbridge had had time to dry in the light of the morning sun, One Who Flies would have had no problems with his footing. But this morning, that was not the case. As his foot slipped, with nothing around to catch, nothing to balance his fall, One Who Flies instantly found himself plunging to the rocky streambed below.

I found myself mesmerized by the story that was being shared with me in my early morning sleep state. My emotion, if there is such a thing as true emotion in sleep, ran the gamut. I had no expectation that, in this first connection, life would end for a person I felt such a strong connection to. That gave me a sense of profound and unexpected loss. The purpose of this was to tell me what? Was this just a story that was to be told through me? It felt like there was more, but this twist wobbled my mind. I felt disturbed by the whole thing.

The connection we shared, which had seemed intriguing just moments earlier, now shifted to a less peaceful energy. The feeling of impending doom overwhelmed my mind and made my heart heavy. A sadness swept over me, and all I could see was the enormous loss that one fateful step had brought for he, his family and his village. I felt the loss as well. What an unusual end to a journey that, if accomplished, could have saved his people, assuming the vision he'd had was true.

"We are connected, and all is well. You are just experiencing the emotion of sudden and unexpected change. You are feeling through me as I felt then. All is well," he spoke with a calm reassurance in his voice that immediately settled my nerves and restored the peace of the moment.

There was more to learn, that much I knew. What seemed the obvious end perhaps was not an end at all. Yet there was still a foreboding feeling of loss that did not just vanish with his words. The connection I felt to him was deep, and as his life was lost, I felt a bit of me die as well.

"We each have a purpose. The fabric of life binds us, each bringing to the tapestry our part to make it beautiful and whole. You and I, are connected, however, in a way that is different from most. You must know, as much as can be revealed, who you are and why you are receiving this message from the mountain. But know, just as the old Shaman did not tell me that I would lose my footing, I cannot reveal to you your destiny, for it is your choices that will create the journey. The outcome is not fixed, but the purpose is clear, and that is why I am here with you now."

"But why did you have to d...?"

Before I could get the question asked, his gentle voice resonated in my head and, in a sense, throughout my body.

"You perceive the outcome one way. What you perceive from an earthly plane as doom or death is nothing more than rebirth—a transformation of sorts. When the old Shaman had accomplished his purpose, when he had planted the seed of truth in me to share with others, he was then free to be born back into life, into all that he connected with. He was free to lose the restrictions that human form required and to find the expansion of who he really was. His death, as you would call it, expanded the energy of his life."

I heard what One Who Flies said. In some ways, I understood. It had been said like that before countless times. Yet, I still could not reconcile how his mission to save his family could end so abruptly without a successful outcome. How could the end of his life in this manner be the fulfillment of his life objective?

I heard his chuckling reply even though my question was never uttered aloud.

"You ask too many questions! Free yourself of your earthly thinking. Close your eyes and ears to thought while you still have the chance this early morning, and allow yourself to feel. Through your feeling, you will find your answers and the peace that you seek."

As his words were completed and resonated in my head, I began to slow and quiet my mind, allowing my heart to feel the experience of the moment. Words fail me as I begin to describe those next moments. It was as if I became One Who Flies, feeling and experiencing the exact sensations he experienced as his footing gave way.

Running onto the footbridge, One Who Flies had no concern over his crossing, knowing that he had done this many times before. Traversing this bridge was natural for him. He had created this shortened path. He had created a way to bridge this gorge just as he created a way to bridge cultures introducing the thought of oneness versus separation.

As his foot slipped and his body entered the unsupported air, at that moment, time stood still, and the question that had gone through his mind as he ran through the night was answered. The Shaman's words—"Know this: even as you run—and run you will, you have done well. Your daughter is part of her father and will pave the way for your mission to continue, whether you do or not." Those words now made sense to him.

Suspended in mid-air, One Who Flies knew that, bound by human form, it would not be natural to quit, to give up, to allow the next phase of life to follow. Life, by its very nature, is bound by natural rules and, like it or not, we have chosen, as we take human form, to play by those rules. In his case, he must give up his human life in order for the next phase of expansion or growth to take place. His vision, destined to come true, was necessary in order for him to make the choice to do what was natural and, at the same time, to position himself to find a natural end. It was his time, and as he was suspended in mid-air he knew that.

Then, I experienced something that was foreign but joyful, abundant and expansive. It was the same feeling that One Who Flies was experiencing that moment his body plunged into the riverbed below. I sensed a golden radiant light that seemed to lift his spirit (and, in a sense, mine as well) out of the confines of human form. The glow was everywhere. There was no place it was not, and it seemed that life teemed with a vibration that welcomed the otherwise disconnected connection. In his body, there was only so much One Who Flies could experience, but as he left his body, he found no boundaries. He was truly one with everything that was around him. Then, with almost a magical explosion of energy, the transformation was complete. Reconnecting with his source—the One—was complete.

He was bathed in love, and this morning, in the time just before dawn, he reached out across space and allowed me to live vicariously through his experience. I, too, felt bathed in love. It was more precious and joyful than I could ever have imagined. I felt loved and adored, a part of everything that was around me. I felt one.

Nestled in the comfort of this early morning bliss, I lay in peace. The joy of oneness was something I relished, knowing soon the morning would come. I was not One Who Flies. My path, yet unrevealed, was still to be completed. But, the journey that had started with the old woman from the mountain had now grown, and, with it, so had I. If I had any trepidation about where this might lead, it was gone as I basked in the warm glow of love.

Chapter Twenty-One

A New Understanding

Throughout this unexpected journey, I have struggled with asking from my head and feeling with my heart. As humans, we see time as linear. We start at the beginning and find the end. Everything seems, from appearances, to be disconnected—separate. Yet, while my head wants to tell me otherwise, I know from the radiant light I experienced with One Who Flies that we are connected in ways we cannot yet imagine.

"Are you now coming to realize who you are?"

Warm and sweet, I would know that voice anywhere. The old woman from the mountain always brought with her a kind gentleness that reminded me so of my early days with my grandmother.

"I wonder," she began to ask, "do you now understand where your fear of heights comes from?"

I could almost hear a chuckle in her voice as she deviated from the more serious side of our communications to one where she now knew I could connect the dots.

"Yes," I replied. "I once had been told that I was a young Indian brave who lost his life in a fall. I could see him lying face down in a river bed. It made some sense then, but never could I have imagined how much more sense it makes now."

I could feel the warmth of her laugh. No reply was necessary. We both had come far, and the depth of our communication and understanding was at a level that transcended outward talk. The sense of fear had dissipated, as I now knew much more about transition, destiny or fate—whatever label we might give it. There is a purpose to what we do and when we do it. It's the journey that makes it fun.

"One Who Flies could not bridge the chasm of understanding between cultures. His daughter, captured in the raid of his village, could. She, like her father, had a purpose, and her purpose was set into motion the day her father died."

The old woman from the mountain's words resonated with truth. Every fiber of my being felt that truth.

"Did One Who Flies choose his end so her beginning could take place?" I knew the answer almost the moment I uttered the question, but I had to ask. Still, the very human side of me—that space between my two ears—wanted to have confirmation of the answer.

"You know the answer, don't you?"

"I think I do. Yes, I believe so."

Then, it was as if she looked right through me, although she wasn't physically present. Her voice was quiet, soothing and gentle, much like the part of the streambed where the water moves along with little effort or strain.

"We all choose our beginnings and our endings. That we do before we get here. But I'm not telling you something that you don't already know. You feel the truth even if it is not spoken."

The next words she spoke were life changing and helped me in the process of finding meaning. They were the last audible words she spoke to me. But then, I did not know that at the time. I do now.

"The daughter of One Who Flies was known as 'Raven' among her captors and newfound family. She was also your great-great-grandmother. Her spirit and playful vitality brought joy to those around her, and her childlike innocence paved the way for new people and cultures in this developing land to come to know truth. She opened a portal of spiritual understanding that was far-reaching. While her memory has all but faded, in her quiet, kind, gentle way she carried the message of the old Shaman further than any of her ancestors could have imagined.

"That message, the one she elected to bring, seems to be all but lost in your generation. The time has come. It is now your time to awaken to your life's purpose."

"Soon you will be introduced to a place of tranquility and beauty, a place where your soul will be nourished. It is a place where the water falls from two places and washes over the mammoth rocks below. Go there and lay on the rocks. Allow the sun to stream across your face. There, you will be cleansed and prepared for the next phase of your journey. There you will receive messages.

"It is now your time. When you see the orange moon banded by clouds in the night sky and lightning illuminating the clouds nearby, you will have been given a sign. Know that all is as it should be. There are no mistakes. Be open to your signs, and follow your path. Now is your time."

Chapter Twenty-Two

Introduced by Chance

"Come with me. I want you to see this property. I'm thinking of either selling it or putting a cemetery on it, and I need your opinion."

The time of talking to the old woman had passed, and the silence seemed deafening. I had begun a new career venture, and my boss had taken me into his confidence and sought my advice on several ventures he was considering. And, as one could imagine, with the beginning of a new venture, my time had become consumed with thoughts of marketing and business growth. The more I became consumed with earthly success, the less I focused on the messages I had received to date.

Of course, when he asked for my help, I was up for the trip.

Months had passed since I had been told by the old woman from the mountain that "it was my time." Nothing. No communication and no signs that I could discern had presented themselves to me. All seemed quiet, and, as days passed, my focus seemed more deeply grounded in the present, in making the new venture successful. The more I thought about the tasks of daily living, the less I thought about the messages that I had been given. This was a time of earthly work, and spiritual thoughts seemed to fade. I suppose one could say I had re-entered "mind sleep."

There is an underlying assumption that focus in the world of business and the development of spiritual practice and growth are mutually exclusive. Is that true? Writing these words, I feel that the answer is "no." Yet I hear a resounding "yes" ringing in the space between my ears. Is "spiritual growth" less connected with daily human endeavors and more connected with the "out there" realm of existence? That question is likely the current modern-day conundrum about the disconnect between daily life and being spiritual.

One Who Flies knew differently. He knew that being present and living was part of his being—his spirit. When he sought food, he was living in Spirit, and he knew that Spirit would meet his needs. He was not disconnected from his source. When he formed shelter from the earth beneath his feet, he thanked Spirit for his protection. As his daily activities were performed, he understood that Spirit was a part of all of life and that one could not disconnect from Spirit. I consciously knew that too. Yet I admit that, as each day unfolded, I was not conscious of the spiritual aspects of my life choices. Perhaps that's part of the mystery of being both spirit and human at the same time. And perhaps one day the five senses will give way to a greater spiritual awakening that allows for us to truly experience the oneness that is very real in each of our lives. Whether or not we choose to believe or experience that oneness, we cannot change its existence.

As I sat in the car, having placed my hiking boots in the back floorboard, I was looking forward to this half-day journey to property that had once been traversed by Native Americans. During our ride, Adam showed me parts of the nearby countryside that was new to my eyes. The feeling was peaceful. There was a connection the closer we came to the mountainous valley property that he now owned. It was much like going back in time as the road became like a ribbon with tight turns that hugged the terrain to either side. Frankly, I was surprised that a paved road existed this far out. I thought to myself, *The government must have needed to spend some money for pavement to be this far out into a land that is little touched by modern civilization.*

"We're almost there," Adam said as we rounded yet another hairpin turn. "We take a left here at 'Splatterhead.'"

I shook my head as I heard his words. "What did you call it?"

"Splatterhead."

"Splatterhead?"

"Yeah, rumor has it that several people who frequented this shanty of a bar were killed by a shotgun blast. So the locals call it 'Splatterhead.' There. There is the bathroom for the bar."

As I looked up, all I could see were two collapsing, weather-worn outhouses. *Surely,* I thought to myself, *he must be kidding.* I couldn't imagine walking in there much less doing my business in those facilities. The more we drove, the more we seemed to be going back in time.

In short order, we were driving along the road perimeter of his property, and by its looks it had not been touched by man in many lifetimes. Rising above the open field—which likely once had been a riverbed rich with earth deposited from the nearby stream—were mountains with mature trees never cut or thinned by the development of man.

As we got out of the car, I placed on my boots, preparing for the trek into the woods that I knew had once been the playground of my ancestors. While we were there for one reason, determining what to do with the property, I knew that there was a reason beyond the obvious for my visit there that day.

Everything happens for a reason. Today was no exception. I admit that, as I began our short hike into the woods, I was not completely conscious of the spiritual reason for being there, but my soul resonated with the ancient connection to this area from generations past. Had I been here before? I couldn't say for sure. But one thing was clear: the more I delved into the woods, the more I was connected with Spirit. The past and connection to Spirit was strong for me there.

As we moved past the expanse of the field into the shadows of the woods, I heard a voice coming from within, prodding me to go deeper.

Not to go deeper into the woods, although that's exactly where we were headed, but to go deeper in my feelings, to allow meaning that was deeper than what appeared on the surface to become part of the experience. It was as if I was being told that here, this day, I was being presented a key. I knew I was to be observant, to be aware. There was a knowing that, as we crossed the bubbling stream, something would be revealed.

It was one of the few times that the message I received was not from another. I heard nothing from the old woman from the mountain or One Who Flies; rather; the voice was an inner voice that was more a feeling than articulated words. Perhaps this represented a shift. Regardless, the vibration of the mountain resonated peacefully in my soul. It felt like home.

There was a sad part to this experience as it unfolded, though. My earthly purpose was to help determine how to convert this land which had a substantial bank mortgage into something that protected the right of the owner at the bank's expense. It felt very much like manipulation and seemed so far removed from the time in the not so distant past when no man owned the land. The land was a gift, and, in harmony, my ancestors shared in its bounty. Now, it has quickly become the foundation of human dispute. Sad!

We walked. It seemed like a mile or two, although in retrospect, it likely was far less. As we moved around trees and under brush and branches that had rarely been touched by man, I heard Adam up ahead say, "Hey, Chuck…it's ahead."

"What?" I called back to him, fifteen or so steps ahead of me.

"This!"

I rounded a large pine tree that had been growing in the forest for many years. Around its massive trunk, I could hear the rushing of water and see the corner of a well-worn building. Immediately beyond it was an awesome natural waterfall.

Somewhere in the past 50 years, man had traversed this pristine wooded area and found the resources and way to build a secluded cabin in the woods just to the left of what was likely a 20-foot waterfall that sent its rushing water down, to the left and around some of the most beautiful rock formations that I had seen in years.

I was in awe. I couldn't believe what had just unfolded before my eyes. I could feel the vibration of the rush of water as it dropped, settled and then twisted its way as it continued on its journey to the waiting river below. The sound of water cascading down the largest of the rocks resonated with a deep voice of power like the timpani, bass and deep tuba sounds of a vast orchestra. Those sounds accentuated the lighter orchestral sounds of settling water and gurgles of the stream as the accumulated water found its way downstream after the exhilarating fall from the massive rock in the center of the falls. It was a sight to behold. All of my senses were tingling with joy as I enjoyed witnessing what was unfolding before me.

I could have stayed there for hours, but just as the feeling seemed to create a wonderful vibrational match, I heard Adam's voice bringing me back to the reality of the moment.

"I'd love to buy this cabin."

I could understand exactly why Adam would say this. The majesty and beauty were quite awesome.

"I feel at peace here," Adam spoke. And it was at that moment that the façade of business seemed to dissipate from his busy exterior, and he let me get just a glimpse of his divinity. I had never heard him speak of peace. His fast–paced and hurried life seemed to resonate anything but peace. But here, right now, the truth of Spirit was revealed.

There is a soft spot, I thought to myself. "Yep," I said, "I can understand why you would want this spot. It oozes peace and tranquility. Time just seems to fade away."

As we moved away from this place, crossing the stream at a narrow point, Adam spoke once again.

"Let me show you something else. If you think this is awesome... well, wait till you see this."

Chapter Twenty-Three

The Prophesy

"Where water falls over two places...." The words that I had heard not so long ago were apparently soon to be fulfilled. As we walked away from the first falls—splendid as they were—I knew that Adam's comment that followed—"let's go to Twin Falls"—referred to the place that I was destined to go. Frankly, I couldn't believe what I was hearing from such an unexpected source.

I had never heard of Twin Falls and I'd had no clue that any place in South Carolina could have the same vibration as what I had felt in the North Carolina mountains. But then, man creates boundaries which Spirit does not. We divide, we sell, we buy, we own. But the vibration of creation has no boundary and cannot be owned.

What was I to witness? The words voiced by the old woman from the mountain seemed straightforward and yet unclear. "Soon, you will be introduced to a place of tranquility and beauty, a place where your soul will be nourished. It is a place where the water falls from two places and washes over the mammoth rocks below. Go there and lay on the rocks. Allow the sun to stream across your face. There, you will be cleansed and prepared for the next phase of your journey. There, you will receive messages." She didn't understand that I was with my boss. How could I lie on the rocks, take in the sun, be cleansed and receive messages? And was this the place?

Traveling a short distance from our former location, again Adam led the way. "This is pretty cool." At times, he overstated reality with a type of optimistic exuberance that I completely understood. In this case, though, his words proved to be an understatement when we crested the hill and the sound of the tremendous waterfalls meant we were near our destination.

"It's just ahead."

I am not normally at a loss for words, but as we walked up the narrow path, a clearing emerged, and before me was "Twin Falls." It was incredible. What seemed well over 75 feet topping the ridge was a spectacular massive dual-pronged waterfall that had a grandeur you would expect to see in a movie. At the top left of this opening expanse was a double stream of water that dropped straight down to a pool below. Energy from the massive falls was absorbed in the wading pool below, and as water cascaded down in a mighty rush, the water resting below was forced over its banks and began again its journey. The mist from the accumulated water seemed to permeate the air with freshness and purity that I've only experienced in the lushness of a mountain tropic. Ten yards to the right, separated by a majestic tree that somehow took root in the granite rock formation separating the two falls, was a cascading waterfall that seemed to have four vertical drops crisscrossing right, then left, then right again. Water from the collecting pool on the left rushed over its holding ridge and tumbled down to meet the waters that rushed down from the right. Together, they formed a type of unity combining the fresh water into a powerful stream bent on finding its way back to its source.

Standing there, I understood at many levels lessons that soon would be revealed. For the moment, I stood in awe of the grandeur that unfolded before me. Not once, but twice in the short span of an afternoon (which had started out as a simple business venture) I had witnessed unexpected beauty and the fulfillment of a promise made— one which I had not understood at the time.

Often, things are not as they seem. A business venture was the veiled cloak of an unfolding opportunity that neither of the players knew was happening. In retrospect, we were both active in the revelation of Spirit, yet neither, if asked, would have had a clue. It seems that often that is the case. What is supposed to happen happens, but the players are so caught up in their roles and in playing them well that they don't grasp the full knowledge that they are in a play.

I knew the time was not right to do as directed—to lie on the rocks, absorb the light, be cleansed and become open to messages. Yet unfolded before me was the material manifestation of a prophecy. Adam played his part perfectly without even knowing that more was happening than a simple walk in nature.

"This is awesome." The words I exclaimed to Adam were stated with humbleness as I kept my eyes on what was before me. As I gazed his way, I could see a grin break out on his face. It was as if our purpose together was to bring me to this point.

"I know," he said with an internal joy that seemed to beam from within. While I was so caught up in experiencing him in the vibration of our material world and business ventures, I found in this moment a glimpse of a more radiant grandeur. I got what I felt was a brief glimpse of his spirit, a spirit that radiated with kindness for others and a deep desire to help others along their path.

As I turned back to the falls, breathing in the increased humidity brought by the power of falling water, I felt the old woman from the mountain again. Our communications were now more a depth of feeling than an audible direction. While I liked the clarity of hearing her as I had at first, the depth of expression seemed more vibrant and clear as messages reverberated throughout my being.

"Come back and step on these rocks. You need time to feel. You've been here before. Come back and remember. Then you'll know the next steps."

I knew what I felt, heard or experienced from my old friend was truth. Where I was felt very familiar. It was as if it had been tucked away, hidden from view, veiled—only to be revealed when the seeker was ready. At that moment, I chuckled internally to myself. *Isn't that just like life? When you least expect it—when you're ready—the teacher will appear.*" Perhaps the physical falls were not there to teach, but what I did know was that there were unseen forces in the mountain that could speak, and the closer I got to the source, the more I felt at ease.

"Go now. Your time has not come. But soon…."

As those words resonated internally, I heard Adam sadly break the surreal silence. "Ready to go? Guess it's time we get back."

What had seemed like a dream when I first began recording my journey was becoming very real. Fact or fiction? Perhaps what appears to be fiction becomes fact. Perhaps fact is created from our state of consciousness. Perhaps my old woman from the mountain was becoming more real than imagined.

I breathed deeply as I began, once again, to follow Adam down the path away from the falls. Looking over my left shoulder, I caught a last glimpse of the location I knew I would be visiting again. Then it struck me as funny—at least internally. *A man I would never have expected,* I thought to myself, *whose name was Adam (first man) has led me to a place I would never have found on my own. Perhaps he is sent to me as my current earthly spirit guide.* Then my earthly consciousness, somewhat ego-centered, welled up, and I thought, *Not Adam!*

Chapter Twenty-Four

A New Perspective

I wanted to plant something. There was a deep longing to establish roots, and with all the moves which had taken place in a simple twelvemonth span, I felt disconnected and detached—a bit like a seed that is blown from place to place, not resting anywhere long enough to blossom into the full majesty of what it could be. Sometimes we just need solitude and a state of quiet reflecting in order to allow the full germination of who we are. If anyone thought they knew me, they would never say I was one to spend my time in quiet contemplation. But then, few knew me.

Perhaps this journey that started so oddly just over a year ago was the beginning of an unexpected transformation. I was not prepared to explain it. All I knew was that each part of it was very real; looking back, it seemed stranger than fiction.

Just over a year ago, when I had heard the mountain speak, my life—at least as I knew it—had dramatically changed. Once again, my choices had been the catalyst for a dramatic shift in my life, one perhaps that, at least on the surface, I did not desire. Strange, but the last time I faced something similar in life, I found a great opportunity for growth in all dimensions. As the initial moments passed, I did not completely recognize a similar pattern unfolding, but in the scope of just over a year I found, once again, that it had. Once again, I had entered into a time of change—change that I now feel is propelling me forward to my life's calling.

It seems that often the choices we make in life which are viewed as obvious mistakes are actually subconscious nudges or urges to move things along—to find the path and, unknowingly, force ourselves to get on with it. While many might disagree, I know that, at least for me, every choice has a consequence, and often those unexpected consequences prove to be the best teachers or stimulants for growth.

While all this may be true, it didn't change the fact that we had moved three times in 14 months covering more than 1800 miles, and I still had no place to plant my roots. I felt that if I could just plant a tree—give a living thing a place it could call home—then maybe I could find a place that could be home to me.

Night was upon me, and outside I heard the drops of rain tapping out a rhythm against the window of my temporary room. It was time to quit writing and drift away into another world. In that time right before deep sleep or early in the morning right before coming into earthly awakening, I often find comfort and messages. Would tonight be one of those evenings or would I just find comfort being nudged to sleep by the constant reminder of the earth around me and Spirit everywhere as the wind carried the rain?

The last thing I recall is the rhythm of life droning away against the pane of my window. Sleep....

Water dropping from the sky—just a tiny drop—yet in that drop is the full majesty of all water. Whether one drop insignificantly falling from the sky or the accumulated drops of water combined to form the ocean, each drop is perfect and just as complete as the vast expanse of all water combined. How appropriate that I fell asleep listening to the gentle patter of raindrops against my window.

"Watch," I heard a new voice say. This voice was one I had not heard before. The sound was not mature and nurturing like that of the old woman from the mountain or strong and powerful like One Who Flies. Rather, this voice seemed playful, spry, full of energy and incredibly youthful—almost like a hummingbird speaking, but clearly a human voice.

"Watch," the voice said. "The drop of rain will fall from the sky and join other drops in the comfortable environment you call a lake. This drop, the one you watched fall from the sky, is at rest lazily floating with other drops together in a place that requires very little effort. There is little there to disturb its peace save for the meandering fish who, breaking the surface in search of food, splash about, creating ripples in the lake.

"This is how you were—comfortably floating with others of your kind, experiencing your humanness and doing little."

I could hear almost a giggle in her voice—well, at least, I think it was a 'her.' "Who are you?" I asked.

"Pay little attention to who I am or where the voice you hear comes from. It is your mind who wants to know. That's not important. It is your heart that needs to hear, and right now you need to focus on that little drop that fell from the sky. Close your eyes. Breathe calmly and notice the drop falling…falling…falling. Tell me what you see?"

"I see a pure, crystal clear drop of water, perfect in every way, no more than the whole, no less than the whole—just sheer perfection."

"Very good," this new entity exclaimed with a tingle of joy that reminded me of a child's experience of Christmas. "Now, when the drop fell into the lake, what did you see? Remember to look closely at your drop."

For a moment, I put my hands to my head, fingers to my eyes and rubbed them. I felt conflicted and confused. I wanted to know who was asking these questions and why now and what for? Rubbing my eyes with my head in my hands, once again I tried to focus on my drop— the one I pictured falling from the sky.

"The drop in its perfection has joined other drops, and together they have found the harmony and rest that this lake provides. Within its bounds, many perfect drops can find a place of comfort and solace.

Together they can 'be!'" As I spoke those words, I realized that we all are in a state of 'being.'

"That's right. Now, quietly close your eyes and allow yourself to float. You'll be safe. You know as you hear my voice that no harm will come to you. After all, you create your existence, so you know that nothing can happen that you don't allow. And you are allowing this—otherwise, I would not be able to talk to you.

"Follow my direction and rise gently—ever so gently—until you can see above the treetops, above the canopy of the forest below. Now tell me what you see."

Amazed by the beauty that could be seen from a different vantage point, I quickly grasped the power that also comes from moving past where we are daily to seeing life from a different perspective. "That little drop—the one you've had me follow from the sky to the lake—the comfort that drop is currently experiencing is soon to be changed."

"Yes." I could hear a smile in her voice a she continued, "And the same is true for you."

Looking above the canopy, I could see that the lake that seemed so peaceful on the surface had an outlet that allowed for few, but enough, droplets to escape. Once that process took place, there was an amazing transformation—one that was powerful enough to change the earth. That little drop resting in the lake—perfect in every way—was soon to join select others in escaping the bounds of daily comfort and become a driving force for change. That drop—my drop—was soon to become the waterfall that had been foretold and that I had recently seen.

"When your drop—the one you saw falling from the sky—joins in the power of movement, there is nothing that can stop it. Its power can carve valleys out of mountains and reshape the world as you know it. So can you!"

Over and over, the word that screamed in my head was "transformation." The once simple water drop that I had captured in my mind's eye as it dropped from the sky was soon to be transformed, combined with other drops on a similar path, into raging waterfalls and a rapidly advancing river using its power to forever change the landscape.

With a brief exhale of air, the almost fairy-like sounding creature said in an airy but clear, youthful voice, "Transformation. That's good. I like that description. Quite clever. Your water drop was whole, perfect and complete as it made its way to join others. You've done the same. Now, it's on a journey of transformation. It will always be whole, perfect and complete, but yet, it will never be the same as its transformation will allow it to become more powerful and to have more influence than many of its kind will ever know. The same is true for you.

"I ask you to look once again. Follow your drop and tell me, does any harm befall it on its journey?"

As I followed the drop—my drop—I noticed the journey was not always comfortable and, at times, could be downright scary. Yet, at no time did any harm befall my drop. At all times, from the majesty and terror of the falls to the power of the rushing stream carving its way through the toughest of ancient rock, my drop was always whole, perfect and complete. It was as if one drop of water contained the power of all water.

"Just as that simple drop of water seemed insignificant as it fell, you now know that it contains the power of all water. What may seem separate from the source nonetheless contains the power of the source. The same is true with you! You are no less than the source, and you have the power to change the world.

"You have been brought to these falls to be told of your transformation. From here, the path will be swift, quick and decisive just like the water falling over the falls. Oh, and there's no turning back. Enjoy the ride, and claim your destiny. You are here for a reason. It is your time."

As I awoke the next morning to the annoying sound of the alarm on my cell phone, I had no recollection of the conversation that later came back to me. That seems often to be the case. I receive a message and then am not aware of its transmission. It takes a trigger to bring it back. Perhaps that's a pattern in life. We walk in a state of unconsciousness, blinded to our true selves, to how whole, perfect and complete we are.

The second trip to Twin Falls triggered my memory and the clarity of vision shared by my newfound friend whom I affectionately call Minerva.

Chapter Twenty-Five

Voices Passing Through

M oments of sheer joy were surrounded by what seemed to be chasms of daily monotony, from the time I was visited by my pixie friend, Minerva, to my next conscious spiritual experience. It seemed like time had wasted away. I had begun to doubt this whole experience. Perhaps it was just the musing of a delusional mind. Perhaps there was nothing special I was to share. Perhaps I should just focus on what was comfortable and let life unfold as it would.

Then they began to happen.

"Be open."

I had just laid down for some much needed rest when, once again, I heard her voice—although this time it didn't seem so playful and pixie-like. The left side of my neck seemed strained, and, as my head hit the pillow, I recall thinking how wonderful it would be to have a gentle neck massage. The voice, however, changed the rest that soon would come.

"Be open. Be attentive. Be receptive."

No words followed, and none were needed. I knew that, with all that had happened along this spiritual journey, the need for elongated explanation was reduced. Expecting the unexpected was becoming quite normal, and, although it had been some time since my last message, hearing or feeling from unexpected sources was becoming quite common and welcome.

I knew exactly what was meant by those three simple commands. For that matter, the messages were a little outdated, so to speak, as serendipitous events had been occurring for some time.

Of course, hearing voices and carrying on "imaginary" conversations was a bit out there. Yet it had become quite acceptable to me and perhaps even normal. In each case, it seemed the voices were directed to me, a way of providing me guidance, gentle nudges designed to move me in the direction of my intended life purpose. So when the voices changed, when they became the channel through which others receive guidance, I was a bit taken aback.

The wheels screeched as we touched down in Providence, Rhode Island. This trip, like others before it, was—on the surface—just another sales training consulting meeting. I must admit I was a bit excited because the engagement was related to radio sales, and I felt at times like a frustrated DJ. So, as you can imagine, the idea of doing work for a radio station had a certain media allure.

Greg was waiting for me at the airport. We had not met prior to my arrival. In fact, the entire engagement had been set up by a connection I'd met through Facebook. Goldie, as she referred to herself, had reached out to me, and we became quick connections and friends. She introduced me to Greg who stepped out on faith in paying my way to work for his station.

A man of large stature, Greg was a very dark skinned African American man with impeccable diction and what seemed to me to be focused attention. In our ride from the airport to his home I found it interesting that he was full of probing questions that had nothing really to do with the reason I thought I was there. His questions had depth and opened the door for the beginning of a deeper discussion of motivations, intentions and the spiritual reason for the work that he did. I couldn't quite put my finger on it, but it was clear that something more significant than a sales call was taking place. What? That was a bit of a mystery to me.

Soon after lunch, Goldie arrived, and she was every bit the free spirit that I had expected. What her real name was, I have no clue. But, sometime in her life she had become known as "Golden Hawk"—Goldie for short.

Honestly, I wasn't sure just what to make of her or the situation. While I was excited about the job, I had some concerns about the outcome since Goldie was anything but a traditional sales person. If you can imagine a Jewish, Native American hippie, you'd have Goldie. Bandana, Hippie attire, Dream Catcher earrings—I was just waiting for her to bust out a joint and start smoking right in the middle of our meeting. Funny, how quickly we make judgments based on what we see.

Goldie's entrance certainly changed the energy that had developed between Greg and me in our short time together. I found it funny, although I did not share it with them—at least not at first. But Goldie was a high-energy full of life hummingbird, flitting from one idea to the next, keeping the room charged with energy. Greg's energy was different—not bad, but clearly less focused and in some ways more intense. The two were co-workers, yet it was clear from the start that there was tension, and I began to sense that my role was not nearly as simple as it had seemed.

We had completed our first day when it happened. Perhaps it had been there all the time, but I can't say I recall the experience being anything like what happened as we began to break for an evening of rest. Having left Greg, Goldie was taking me to the hotel that was my home for the next week. As we arrived at the front entrance, I heard the voice as clear as music playing through headphones.

"I have some questions for you," I said to Goldie in a somewhat quiet, calming voice. The words that I spoke to her were literally being spoken to me (by whom I don't know), and I felt like an audible microphone repeating what I was hearing.

"You have asked me here for reasons other than what appears on the surface."

As those words were uttered, Goldie took on a "deer in the headlights" kind of look. It seemed that for an instant she stared right through me almost as if she had seen a ghost. Her expression and energy softened as she spoke the last words we exchanged that night.

"I don't know why you are here. I was just told to bring you."

Looking back at her, I knew that it was time to part and that something quite unique was set to unfold. Without as much as saying "Goodbye," I opened the door and left her presence. I was not troubled by what I had heard in my head and repeated to Goldie. Rather, I was taken aback by how clear the voice and message was. It was as if someone higher than I knew a larger picture of what, why and how I was there. I was just a conduit for the message to be delivered. That, I must admit, was unique for me.

I was accustomed to being in control mostly through my intellect. I would rather think from my head than feel with my heart—what I called "mind sleep" not so long ago. Rarely, if ever, did I feel led by a force outside of my control.

Over the course of the next two to three days, I spent time with Goldie and Greg. And during that time, we rarely talked about radio sales or marketing. In fact, I don't recall that conversation lasting thirty minutes at the most. Our discussions centered more on their interests, motivations, goals and dreams.

I have come to believe that "success"—and I use that term loosely—comes when we move in the direction of our dreams. When our focus is aligned with our soul's desire, the path to joy is easy. We can fight our soul's longings, endeavoring in tasks that provide anything but joy, and generally will fail to achieve true fulfillment. On the other hand, when we align our soul's desire with our earthly actions and activities, we come to find fun in everyday life. Work is play, and all is aligned with why we are here, who we are 'being' and our life's purpose.

On what everyone thought was our next to last day together, I found myself listening to Goldie as she curled up in a chair in my hotel room. For several days, she, for no reason she could think of, felt the need to share some of the most intimate parts of her life—some good, but most not so pretty. Abuse, drugs and misguided conduct; I felt like a therapist—and that certainly was not my calling.

"I don't know why I'm telling you this," Goldie blurted out in a moment when she was feeling unusually vulnerable. "Is there something happening here…something you're supposed to tell me?"

Without warning, and certainly with no premeditation on my part, I received a message and almost instantly shared it with Goldie.

"Today is my last day here. My work is done." Those comments were unexpected, especially by me, as my flight was still two days away. Changing my ticket and leaving early was not something that I did when engaged in a consulting relationship. I had no intention of leaving, but it was almost as if I had little control over my mouth—or what came out of it.

"I have come here to share with you that you need to leave the radio station—leave Greg—and find your own way. Your time has come. It is time to move in the direction of your dreams. My role here has nothing to do with radio sales. It does have everything to do with you. You are loved!"

As those words left my lips, I could see the tears well up in her eyes. It was as if I was lifting some burden from her shoulders—giving her permission to do what she already knew needed to be done. My role? I was just the messenger. In the arena of non-physical reality, I had my first experience as a channel sharing a message. My role was nothing more than that of a guide sent to help illuminate the path of an immortal soul whose purpose was to help others.

After our talk, I asked Goldie, "How about giving Greg a call? I'd like to talk to him as well." Goldie complied, knowing that their friendship would last but that their work together was done. And when Greg arrived, much like with Goldie, it seemed I had a message for him which was, again, a confirmation of what his soul knew but his earthly intellect was unwilling to accept.

Greg knew that his message, relayed through me, was to release those chains that had bound him, opening the opportunity for his soul to find the path that would bring help to others and joy to himself. And for me—well, it was an experience I would not forget.

After changing my flight, I left early the next morning to travel back home. Now, I can sleep on an airplane. When they shut the door and those engines send the plane racing down the runway, I can be fast asleep in minutes, especially when the flight is at the crack of dawn. I began to recline my head (as much as you can in that uncomfortable position). But before the chance of sleep came, I felt her old comforting familiar voice, the old woman from the mountain.

"You did well."

I can't tell you how comforting it was to hear her voice. It had been a while and, while I knew she was never far, I had wondered if we'd have more conversations. Her past direction had come true in ways I still did not completely understand. I trusted her with every fiber of my being. She was indelibly a part of me, and just the feeling of her voice brought a calm that changed every fiber of my being.

"From where you were to where you are has been a remarkable transformation. But remember, it is a journey, this thing we call life. Soon, you will come to recognize and openly use what you experienced over the past several days. Just as one of your spirit guides, when I share with you, you will be used as a voice to share with others. That is part of your life's work. Be open and receptive. Now, get some sleep."

The next sounds I heard were the wheels screeching as we touched down in Charlotte.

Chapter Twenty-Six

Finding Your Path

Almost two years ago, this journey began. I recall its beginning as if it were just last week. Awakened from sleep that night, I quietly crept down the creaky stairs of the house we were renting, fired up the laptop and began writing in the dark of night. I didn't know why I was being led to do this and had never thought of such a task, so the concept was strange at first.

The first words of this book just flowed. My fingers moved effortlessly across the keyboard, and as I sat there in the dark of night, before me were words which flowed into sentences and then into paragraphs. After what seemed like minutes, which actually was two hours, the first two chapters were finished. When the message that had started was done—at least for that night—I closed my laptop and went back to bed feeling satisfied and complete.

That's how the process began, and it's been that way ever since. With each keystroke, the story unfolded and the journey continued. I had no outline, no thought of what would take place next, no preconceived notion of what the message was or what meaning it had for me or anyone else, for that matter. All I knew was that I was to write what I received and that the next steps would be revealed in their own time.

At first, and probably more times than not, I have wondered where the story was going, what it meant and where it would end. But then, I have not been in control of the story or the journey; rather, I have been a scribe, using my fingers and the magic of technology to bring into manifestation the reality of a journey that has more meaning than I can comprehend. Sometimes it's best to listen. Then the fog of illusion can lift, revealing the majesty of what lies ahead.

Tonight, as I felt led to write yet once again—thinking that surely there were more chapters and some dramatic ending in store—I felt her voice...the voice that nurtured my soul and provided comfortable guidance with sprinkles of love that touched my soul.

"You've done well."

The old woman from the mountain was speaking as I sat quietly, listening to the sound of rain to my right and watching the flickering glow of a candle on my left. I sat for a moment and experienced the gentle flow of water, hearing it as it slapped the leaves that provided a canopy of cover for the ground below. With eyes closed, I knew that each water droplet was perfect and on its journey to transformation. When I opened my eyes, I saw the burning flame flickering as if to dance in the night with joy knowing that it, too, was part of a transformation that was taking place. Transformation was everywhere. Then, in the quite of my room, my fingers again began to move, much like they had that first night. I was a conduit for what was to come next—her words.

"Your journey is not done, but you know that. There is little now that I can tell you that you don't already know—at least at some level. You have come far and we, your spirit guides and teachers, are rejoicing in your awakening. You have no idea the joy it brings us to see life unfolding into potential—into the purpose which you chose so long ago. This is but one of your transformations. But don't become complacent. There is much work ahead for you—individually and in working with others. You are now awakening and unfolding into your life's purpose."

As I heard her words, I felt the love of her spirit move like currents through my being. Her depth of love was joyful, fulfilling, rich, and enfolding—much like going home to Spirit might feel—at least as much as we here in this earthly plane can feel "home."

"Do you recall one of my first questions to you?"

I had to chuckle and grin when I heard the old woman ask what seemed to be a foolish question. When she had first asked it, so many months ago, I'd had no clue what was taking place, much less what she might ask. At first, I had been taken aback by the odd process of what I'll call "directed typing," so it was all new as it unfolded. But that question…well….

"Of course I do. You asked, 'Who are you?'"

"And what is your answer today to that question asked so many months ago?"

Unlike before, when I had rapidly begun to move into my head to search to find an answer, I knew instinctively the answer. It just felt right.

"I am!"

"That's right. You are and always have been."

The old woman continued in a gentle manner that resonated with a loving tone that felt like a well-worn blanket providing warmth for a lifetime. "So now the question is not 'who are you?' Rather, the question is what are you going to do with who you are?"

As she asked her question, I was instantly transported back to my last time with the old Shaman. Then, a transformation, an awakening of sorts, was taking place—obviously one of many that have become part of the journey. He spoke the following words:

"Your message of light must go beyond those in your tribe. You will infuse your being into all that surrounds you. The power you will share will go beyond any earthly action you take. The wave of light you will broadcast will be received by others you draw to you, and the message will go forth in ways yet to be seen."

Like One Who Flies back then, I was not yet attuned to the meaning in the message when it was delivered, and perhaps today the power of its meaning is yet to be understood. But something inside of me knows that a large part of my life's journey is to be a messenger—to fulfill the agreement that began long ago, way up on the mountain.

Again, her voice resonated throughout my being, "I have one more thing to share with you, my precious one. This message that you have so carefully written down is not only for you, but for all those who read or are touched by these words. Each of you has a special life purpose. While your journey may be different and the path may not be the same, know that you are special and an integral part of the tapestry of this moment in your spiritual journey called 'life.'"

"You have awakened from your 'mind sleep.' Now go help others do the same."

As I heard her last words, I knew that they wouldn't be the last. From deep within my heart, I knew that the journey was really just beginning. The water droplet joined with the lake had just now crossed over the precipice, and the pace and power of the journey was rapidly picking up speed and momentum.

Flashing before my eyes were all those involved in the journey thus far—each knowing that they had played their integral part to get us to where we are right now. So the story has no end. Rather, from this moment forward, the journey continues into the spiritual unfolding of...

"I Am"!

About the Author

You may have seen Chuck on television or heard him on CNN, CBS or NPR radio programs. His **business and personal insights** are sought after for his strong position on ethics, leadership and spiritual growth. **Chuck Gallagher's focus is business—but his passion is empowering others.** His unique presentations clearly demonstrate he brings something to the platform that isn't often found in typical motivational speakers. Chuck's personal experience in building businesses and successful organizations provides a practical and powerful framework for success. But beyond his work in the present, Chuck shares his deep personal connection with Spirit to connect the dots for individuals and organizations alike in ways that have been described as "amazing"—"inspirational"—"meaningful," and the list continues.

Currently COO of a national company and former Sr. VP of Sales and Marketing for a public company, Chuck may have found a sales niche early on in life selling potholders at age 9 door to door, or convincing folks to fund a record album of his musical performance at age 16 (and yes, those were the days when an album was made of vinyl), but it was the school of hard knocks that provided a fertile training ground for Chuck's lessons in success and deepened his connection to Spirit. Described as creative, insightful, captivating, and a person who "Connects the Dots" between behavior, choices and success, Chuck Gallagher gives his clients what they need to turn concepts into actions and actions into results.

In the middle of a rising career, Gallagher lost everything because he made some poor choices. He has since rebuilt his career and his life back to immense success. With more vulnerability than the average keynoter, Gallagher shares with his audiences his life journey, the consequences of his unethical choices, and how life gives you second chances when you make the right choices. In fact, Gallagher's book—**<u>SECOND CHANCES: Transforming Adversity into Opportunity</u>**—has received numerous endorsements and has been described as one of those rare books that effectively bridges the gap between personal accountability and success. Others have described it as Spirit working through the written word connecting with that deep place within each of us that opens us to learn more about what it really is we are here to do.

On a nationwide basis, Chuck has helped countless individuals on their journey to success and heightened spiritual connection! Allow Chuck's story to awaken you to **your** life's purpose.

For more information about Chuck Gallagher visit http://chuck gallagher.com or to contact Chuck email him at chuck@chuck gallagher.com or call him at 1-828-244-1400.